Average to ACES

Sharing Lives, Living Better Lives

JANSON YAP

PARTRIDGE

Copyright © 2020 by Janson Yap.

ISBN:	Hardcover	978-1-5437-5688-3
	Softcover	978-1-5437-5686-9
	eBook	978-1-5437-5687-6

All rights reserved. No part of this book may be used or reproduced by any means, graphic, electronic, or mechanical, including photocopying, recording, taping or by any information storage retrieval system without the written permission of the author except in the case of brief quotations embodied in critical articles and reviews.

Because of the dynamic nature of the Internet, any web addresses or links contained in this book may have changed since publication and may no longer be valid. The views expressed in this work are solely those of the author and do not necessarily reflect the views of the publisher, and the publisher hereby disclaims any responsibility for them.

Print information available on the last page.

To order additional copies of this book, contact
Toll Free 800 101 2657 (Singapore)
Toll Free 1 800 81 7340 (Malaysia)
orders.singapore@partridgepublishing.com

www.partridgepublishing.com/singapore

Contents

About the Author xi
Foreword xiii
Acknowledgements xvii
Prologue xix

1. A Story to Be Told 1
2. A Decade of Digital and Applied Technology 5
3. More Personalisation in a Hyper-Connected Decade 23

SHARING LIVES

4. Amazing ACE 37
5. Sisters' Company 47
6. Painting Your Own Rainbow 70
7. All It Takes Is the First Break 85
8. Dare to Pursue 100
9. Copy Warrior Secrets 118
10. Purpose, Peace, and Progress 129

LIVING BETTER LIVES

11. Average to ACES 147
12. I Am Ready for MORE 174

Appendix 193
References 195
Index 199

Past learnings are good teachers for present-day decisions,
which set up future success.

—Janson Yap

Today's hindsight can be judged against yesterday's foresight.
Today's foresight and insights may impact tomorrow's
hindsight. . . . Therefore, it is important to look ahead to stay ahead.

—Janson Yap

平步青雲

A Gadwise Investments P/L Production

Executive Producer: Janson Yap

Dr. Janson Yap
Average to ACES
I am Ready for MORE

Dr. Lim Cheok Peng
Awesome ACE

Lyddia Cheah
Soniia Cheah
Sisters' Company

Noah Tan
Painting Your Own Rainbow

Kent Tonscheck
All It Takes is the First break

Daphne Ng
Dare to Pursue

Gao Li
Purpose, Peace and Progress

Ange Dove
Copy Warrior Secrets

Special appearance:
Rosyniah Wang is Noah Tan's mother

Cover Design:
Rudy Tedja

About the Author

Dr Janson Yap
*Entrepreneur, business leader,
transformer, author, academic*

Janson is a management and risk advisory consultant providing guidance and assistance on strategic risk matters to the boards and senior management of a diverse range of institutions and business organisations. Contemporary issues have extended his expertise in research and solutions development in various risk categories including brand and reputation, conduct, cyber and regulatory risks. Embedding the innovation culture into the DNA of the Deloitte Southeast Asia organisation is also part of his business portfolio.

He practised as a management consultant for over eleven years at Arthur Anderson, PWC and Deloitte prior to his focus on risk advisory services and consultancy in the past decade. His career in professional services spans over twenty-one years. Prior to joining the professional services industry, he held senior management positions in the corporate sector at Avon Cosmetics, CSR Group, and Estee Lauder Australia Pty Ltd.

Janson's journey of continuous learning has helped him understand and contribute his insights on business strategy and operations through the closed-loop learning of how researched knowledge (theory) informs practice and in turn how actual practice refines theory. His tertiary-learning journey is totally Australian, leveraging the country's rich and proud heritage in education. Beginning in Victoria, Janson completed his Bachelor of Science and DipEd qualifications from Monash University. He subsequently completed his company-sponsored executive MBA from the prestigious Australian Graduate School of Management (AGSM) at the University of New South Wales. He has always been concerned about the high-failure rate of strategy implementation in businesses and went on to conduct advanced research into strategy implementation, earning him a doctorate of professional studies qualification from the University of Southern Queensland. He completed a programme conducted by INSEAD on Strategy in the Age of Digital Disruption to prepare for the impacts of Industry 4.0. He frequently shares his work at seminars, media interviews, and keynote addresses at various international forums. He has authored many articles on business transformation, medical tourism and more recently co-authored a book with Professor Luke van der Laan on *Foresight and Strategy in the Asia Pacific*. He has authored other publications including 'Wow! How did you know that?' and his autobiography.

His passion outside work is in property development, musical compositions, and film. For exercise and relaxation, he jogs and plays badminton. Janson's understanding of the Christian faith is enhanced by his Diploma of Biblical Studies from Moore Theological College, Newtown, New South Wales, Australia.

Foreword

Leesa Soulodre
Entrepreneur / business leader, academic

There is a Chinese saying, '*Tai Shang Yi Fen Zhong, Tai Xia Shi Nian Gong*' (台上一分鈡, 台下十年功). The translation states that a single minute on stage often needs ten years of preparation. Clearly, the minute of fame when accolades of success resound are often preceded by years of diligent effort, perseverance, and resilience.

In my career as a serial entrepreneur, venture capitalist, management consultant, and adjunct professor, I have observed thousands of students, entrepreneurs and executives across the world that aspire to transform themselves professionally and *grow rich*. However, richness is a term, not denoted by money.

Nursing palliative care patients in my youth, I learned quickly that it never matters how much money we have. At the end of our lives, we only care about the quality of the relationships we have or have had with those we love and the impact of our legacy borne from our individual *significance*. I have also learned from my students, my founders, my clients, and in my very own journey, that the most powerful motivator in our lives is never money. Rather it is that opportunity to learn, to grow in our careers and responsibilities, the opportunity to contribute to our families, our communities, to serve others, and to be recognised for our achievements.

But too often in an Instagram world, society focuses us on what we need to *have*, rather than what we need to *be* in order to *do*. Within these chapters, Janson has captured the significance of those within our communities, who personify those years of diligent effort, perseverance, and resilience. Stories like those of Ken, Noah and Dr Lim, or the celebrity Cheah sisters, and indeed, Janson's very own journey, serve to refocus us on the correct formula – that of pondering who we should *be* and what that gives us the social licence to *do* and thereby to *have* – the *riches* that we receive. These champions have *rich lives* and through the telling of their tales, both enrich and humble our very own.

Janson and his selected contributors are indeed role models in our community, that amidst a tidal wave of information, and in only 1,440 minutes in a day, often go unnoticed or underappreciated. Their daily journeys as educators, mentors, visionaries, muses, and champions provide a platform for recognition through sharing their stories.

Janson's many books are a product of his passion for research, learning, and insights gained both as a practitioner and academic, and this one is no different. Janson shares his accumulated wisdom of operating in the business world and stories that share the integrity and empathy that comes from his servant leadership. Janson's insights shared through the pages of ACES are the result of deep technical expertise and relevant international experience, key characteristics of a valued professional in any environment of providing trusted advice to clients' needs.

'Be Yet Wiser' was the motto of Janson's secondary school, a mantra that he has lived and served others by, throughout his illustrious career. Without doubt, one needs to be wiser than ever before in this constantly changing, friction-free economy.

ACES is an outstanding result of Janson's ambition to realise his lifelong dream: that of being a valuable contributor and a successful and authentic leader. ACES serves as a book of our time, and as a role model to remind us of all the real reasons *why*.

Leesa Soulodre MBA MiM
General Partner, R3i Ventures LLC
Managing Partner, RL Expert Group Limited
Adjunct Faculty Member, Singapore Management University, IE Business School.
Singapore, 2020

Acknowledgements

First and foremost, I wish to acknowledge the cast of this Average to ACES production. Dr Lim, Lyddia, Soniia, Noah, Kent, Daphne, Ange and Gao form the main cast, and I thank them for their willingness to share their stories. Knowing them personally adds to the authenticity and richness of the details penned in these stories. Their lives have encouraged me in one way or another.

The support and encouragement of our families and friends have been crucial and sustaining presence since we embarked on this project. It has given us the much-needed motivation to continue researching and writing the various chapters when other demands on time have been equally pressing. Their unstinting and sustained commitment is gratefully acknowledged.

Maintaining physical wellness has become a very important topic for all workers of all ages in these uncertain times. I am grateful to my medical coach, Dr Alvin Ng, who guides and helps me maintain my wellness so that I can continue my daily activities across the various continents. Thanks also are due to Kenny Goh, my physical coach, who has faithfully discharged his duties to help me enjoy and relax at our weekly badminton sessions while improving my fitness throughout these years.

A book is incomplete without a proper foreword. I am honoured that Ms Leesa Soulodre agreed to pen the foreword for this book. She has found time in a busy schedule to gracefully read the manuscript and pen the words.

The last mile of this project is to take this manuscript through to publication. My thanks to Ms Ange Dove who doubles up as editor for bringing this book to life in addition to sharing her story.

This book is dedicated to all who are thinking about their life journeys and working towards their success and significance. Last but not least, I wish to thank my God and Saviour, the Lord Jesus Christ, who has enabled me to live a fulfilled lifestyle, balancing many demands on a daily basis.

Prologue

In chapter 3 verse 1 of the holy book of Ecclesiastes, it says that there is a time for everything and a season for every activity under the heavens. I have written books previously about business, strategy, and the evolution of risks management. I also wrote my autobiography, which was published for private circulation only. Now I feel it is time for an inspirational book – a book that promises hope for all and encourages readers to reach their own North Star and live a full and complete life up to retirement and beyond as ACES.

Inbuilt in us all is the instinctive desire to become successful and respected. No one commences in life by aiming to be a failure. Yet many people fail to achieve their potential in life. This book is about how ordinary folks like you and I, regardless of background and heritage, can become successful and achieve significance in life.

The selected stories in this book reflect the inclusiveness and diversity agenda that has taken centre stage in today's society. Our heroes are from diverse backgrounds, and both genders are included in good balance. Each person featured has achieved their own success and transformation, and they should be proud of their achievements.

The human race is resilient. Human civilisations have progressed through the ages, overcoming forces of change that have brought about technological advancements and social progress. The world has seen four industrial revolutions to date. The era of the *First Industrial Revolution,* commencing in 1760 to about 1820–40, moved production methods from hand to machines. *The Second Industrial*

Revolution, beginning in 1850, championed new types of innovations and manufacturing methods for mass production. This involved the steel manufacturing industry and the chemical, petroleum and automotive industries in the 20th century. This confluence of centralised electricity, the oil era, the introduction of the automobile and suburban construction during the 20th century marked this revolution. Beginning in the 1950s, the *Third Industrial Revolution* brought semiconductors, mainframe computing, personal computing and the Internet to bear, marking the era of the digital revolution. Academics and researchers point to a new era and another industrial revolution. The *Fourth Industrial Revolution*, which made its debut in the second decade of the millennium, builds on leveraging the power of the Internet era and enters into a new phase of cyber-physical systems. The world is at a crossroads once again.

Each era features its own complexities and challenges, but with that comes opportunity. The uniqueness of this present era is the rapid advancement of technological developments and how humans can cope, work, coexist, and benefit by collaboratively working with the technological-digital revolution.

The more informed people are, the better prepared they are to take advantage of the future. They must continuously adapt and upgrade their skills to be relevant in the new world. Just as past generations have adapted to the changes from previous revolutions and the current generation continues to progress and expand, I hope that my readers will find these stories inspiring, learn from them, and apply the lessons in their respective lives and be successful in tomorrow's world.

The key to this is holding the ACES card, a passport of hope. ACES is the acronym for Acceleration, Creativity, Excellence, and Significance. All are positive words and carry the meaning of hope. May you ace in life.

ACES
Acceleration. Creativity. Excellence. Significance.

ACES and My World Stage

My good friend penned these four Chinese words 平步青云 (Píngbùqīngyún) when writing this book. The phrase means small and ordinary steps (even steps). Those I have taken over the years have helped propel me to ACES and prominence (clouds). In order to assess whether achievements are ACES, I developed a set of criteria to assess them:

- Do they fulfil dreams and passions?
- Do they create or capture value as per life's mission?
- Can the values and benefits be shared for the greater good?
- Do others judge the achievements as great? (Wow, you aced this!)
- Will they create a better future – legacy?

In the chapters that follow, there are examples of our heroes who have conquered their failures and limitations and aced in their endeavours. The tables you will find after each of their stories will help you to appreciate how they have applied the five criteria in their lives to take them from average to ACES.

1.0

A Story to Be Told

#To Each His Own

All the world's a stage,
And all the men and women merely players;
They have their exits and their entrances;
And one man in his time plays many parts,
His acts being seven ages.

—Williams Shakespeare[1]

All human beings are actors and play out their own stories on their own world stage. Although all humans have the same biological make-up, no two lives are the same. Each human, regardless of race, age, religion, ethnicity, and background, has his or her own story. There are 7.53 billion stories living across 195 known countries across planet Earth. China and India combined account for over three billion stories.

History is the past documented and the study thereof. Some have defined history as the study of past events, particularly human affairs. History, taught in schools as a subject, serves to help students

---

1 https://www.brainyquote.com/quotes/ William_shakespeare_166828.

understand the perspectives and events of the world and country – political and social affairs. Famous people, including politicians, celebrities, business elites, and iconic leaders have their stories told through their autobiographies. The stories of most heads of state and presidents have been researched and published at some point.

In an attempt to record their stories, most people, at one point or another, have kept a diary or journal. However, unless the individual is disciplined and diligent, such practices rarely last throughout their life and their recordings are neither shared nor published. Most of the hand-me-down stories in families are reliant on memories, supported by some artefacts and pictures. The problem with this is that when recollection and memory fail, the perspectives and truths are sometimes misrepresented or distorted.

As my children grow up and begin to choose their vocations, careers, and lifestyles, they are also settling in different countries. What was once an easy task in gathering the family together for a meal and holiday has become a bit of a logistical challenge in the coordination of everyone's schedules and availability.

Like most fathers, I want my memories shared with future generations as I remember them. I undertook the task to write my autobiography, complete with selected pictures. My story may not be read by many or become a bestseller, but I am proud of this product. Family and friends who have read the book have been impressed, and they applauded the effort. I was able to include a chapter on my ancestral heritage based on my brother's work on tracing our family tree from the time of the Yap's migration from China.

The journey of writing my story was filled with moments of doubt, frustration, happy reflections, satisfaction, and meaning. It took some time to start the project, but once it was underway, it was not as daunting as I had previously envisioned.

In the coming chapters, you will be treated to the stories of different actors on their own stage. I start with the story of Dr Lim, a celebrated cardiac consultant whose story is one of an amazing ace. A man of humble beginnings, his passion is to improve the delivery of healthcare, and he achieved that vision by pioneering patient-centric, research-led healthcare. In his distinguished career, he served as chairman at China Medical & HealthCare Group Ltd, managing director and director at IHH Healthcare Bhd president and chief executive officer at Parkway Group Healthcare Pte Ltd and executive vice chairman and managing director at Parkway Holdings Ltd.

There are two separate stories of female professional athletes, the Cheah sisters and Daphne. These stories spell out their journeys as international competitive players from training and schooling days to career choice, transitions, and life after they peak in their competitive careers. Lyddia, the elder of the Cheah sisters, has since moved on to study and prepare for her next career. Soniia, the younger of the two, is still representing the country and competing internationally. Her story is one of sacrifice and dedication to reach her ambition to compete at international levels. Despite severe injuries that eliminated her from the competitive circuit for a few golden years, her tenacity in chasing her dream saw her mount her comeback to become Malaysia's number 1 female singles player. In a different story, Daphne has left the competitive circuit and is pursuing both academia and business ventures. She has successfully transitioned, is succeeding in business and has just been signed as brand ambassador for Milo.

Noah is an autistic kid. His story is about how society, family, and corporations can rally together and help a young man succeed. His journey is a mixture of heartache, hope, relief, and support.

Ken, a farm boy from the Australian outback is en route to becoming a musician singer, the first in the family to pursue his dream outside of the family norm of farming and raising cattle. His story bears resemblance to those of many celebrities in search of that first break.

Ange collaborates with me on some of my writing. She is the keyboard and copy warrior, who has determination to succeed whatever the odds. Her journey has taken her from starting a business by accident to managing her business leveraging today's and future digital infrastructure. She started Singapore's first and longest-standing copywriting company with no business knowledge and, over time and through experience, has gained the business acumen needed not only to manage and keep the business going but to leverage Cloud technology solutions to keep it lean and ready for the way business will be conducted in the future.

One of my mentees is Gao Li. Born in China, he moved to Singapore at the age of seven and grew up as a migrant child. He shares his story of adaptation and social acceptance, as well as some of the mistakes he has made in building relationships and looking for that North Star. In some ways, his journey is not too dissimilar from many of us and we can learn from it.

Last, but not least, is my story. Armed with a dream, I have journeyed from being an unknown boy in a big family from a rough neighbourhood and have progressed well in my corporate, professional services, and entrepreneurial careers, having tried my hand at many things.

Let us begin.

2.0

A Decade of Digital and Applied Technology

#Defining Moments

The decade starting in 2010 gained momentum and truly ushers us into the era of the digital revolution, which is set to revolutionise and transform future societies and generations.

Like any other decade, 2011–2019 has revealed historic events, celebrations of joyous outcomes and significant grief brought about by disasters and conflict. I see this decade as a period of defining moments as we cross the threshold of the physical and industrial age into the digital era. There has been much progress, and many inventions and developments, some welcome and others not. It is time to take stock of the decade and draw on the many lessons we can learn from the events that have occurred.

Back in December 2009, an article was published entitled 'The 2000s: A Decade of Doom or Diversions?' The author was trying to reflect on the happenings of the decade that was ending. I write this chapter with the same intention to reflect on the happenings within the closing decade so that one can be more prepared for the next.

I recall conducting an experiment at a company town-hall meeting, where staff were asked to list the ten highest and lowest points of the previous ten years and what they thought would be the important milestones and happenings in the coming ten years. The exercise highlighted that most people could list two or three at the most, and in the second exercise, they were not able to list anything extraordinary in terms of being prepared or what the future holds for them.

Having reviewed the decade in question, I see it as the *digital- and applied-technology decade.* Many factors in this decade and the one before it contributed to new business trends all over the world. These factors have brought about significant change in output and business processes in general, resulting in the changed business, political, and social ecosystems and landscapes we live in today.

This chapter lists several major themes/insights:

- learnings from two natural disasters – Japan and US
- world leaders, legacy, contributions, and records
- new winners in the business league table
- the arrival of the digital age and next industrial revolution
- sharing economy
- consequences of greed, sub-prime mortgages, and the housing crisis
- lessons from financial crises
- a lost decade for Americans

Each of these themes and insights is described in the remaining pages of this chapter, in no particular order of importance.

BAU and Extraordinary Events

Even with the disruptions, changes, and transformations happening around us, a large proportion of the population takes a business-as-usual (BAU) approach to living. They wake up in the morning and go through the motions. As change happens, they adapt.

A small proportion are directly affected by the changes, with some facing more challenges than others. There are the game changers such as technopreneurs who have driven change in the ecosystem with their new business and operating models through their digital-human platforms. Education systems are also changing and adapting. Family and personal budgets are becoming increasingly stretched with the rising cost of living, punctuated by employment disruptions in some cases.

Those who are cognisant of the technology trends leading the transformation find adoption, for the most part, to be slower than expected while some technologies such as the smartphone, conversely, have quickly been ingrained into our daily lives. The point is that the change is uneven, and this is typical of transition from the physical to the digital era.

Humanitarian and Economic Crises Resulting from Japan's Tsunami and Nuclear Disaster

Nature has its say every so often in our history. The start of the digital- and applied-technology decade was negatively impacted when Japan's north eastern shoreline was hit by a 100-foot tsunami following an earthquake of 9.0 magnitude[2] and caused ripples across the world. Fukushima Nuclear Plant suffered damage during the tsunami, which caused radioactive leaks, resulting in the loss of about 19,000 lives and much damage to coastal ports and towns. Over a million buildings were destroyed or partly collapsed[3]. The shutdown of Japan's supply of nuclear energy caused a slowdown in the global economy. This was clearly a black-swan event, a rare, low-probability, unanticipated occurrence with enormous ramifications.[4]

---

2 E. Kamarck, 'The fragile legacy of Barack Obama', *Boston Review, April 2018*.
3 'World Nuclear Association', 2018, https://www.world-nuclear.org/information-library/safety-and-security/safety-of-plants/fukushima-accident.aspx.
4 Yap and Nones, 'Wow! How did you know that?', 2018.

A summary of the findings and recommendations on lessons learned from the Fukushima accident are outlined below[5]:

- Seek out and act on new information about hazards
- Improve nuclear plant systems, resources, and training to enable effective ad-hoc responses to severe accidents
- Strengthen capabilities for assessing risks from beyond-design-basis events
- Further incorporate modern risk concepts into nuclear safety regulations
- Examine offsite emergency response capabilities and make necessary improvements
- Improve the nuclear safety culture

Attention to risk management is still key to mitigating such large-scale black-swan events as, when they do happen, the impacts are significant and long term.

Impactful $180 Billion Damage from US Hurricane Harvey

On 25 August 2017, Hurricane Harvey hit Texas, causing damage of $125 billion[6], more extensive than any other natural disaster in the history of the United States, with the exception of Hurricane Katrina back in 2005. Following his briefing to President Trump, Governor Greg Abbott told reporters, 'We are ready, we are taking steps on a daily basis to make sure we will be able to address any challenge coming our way.'[7] It is good to see that we have learned from previous tragedies and disasters and are prepared for future calamities.

---

5   National Academy of Sciences, 2014.
6   Amadeo, Kimberly 'Hurricane Harvey Facts, Damage and Costs', 2019.
7   Svitek, 2018.

Limited Legacy of Once the Most Powerful Man in the World

Barack Hussein Obama II was the 44th president of the United States and served two terms in office from 2009–2017. He was the first African American elected to the presidency. Obamacare was his major legislative achievement, but critics labelled it a fragile legacy. Kamarck quoted Zelizer, who assessed Obama's presidency, concluding he was a very effective policymaker but not a tremendously successful party builder.[8]

Obamacare is the Affordable Care Act, which was signed into law by President Obama back in 2010 in an attempt to overhaul the health insurance system. Those not covered at work can buy a health insurance plan from a government-run marketplace called an 'exchange', which offers consumers and small businesses a choice of standardised and heavily regulated health plans.[9]

This law was meant to allow millions of *near-poor* Americans to join Medicaid through the exchanges.[10] It is estimated that over 20 million people had received healthcare coverage under Obamacare by 2014.

Any national healthcare system is expensive to maintain. Obamacare is paid for by a combination of government spending cuts and new revenue sources, including tax increases. According to the Congressional Budget Office's (CBO) estimates, US$700 billion spending will be trimmed by 2025 through cuts in Medicare payment rates and reductions in payments to the Medicare Advantage Program under the Obamacare scheme. On the revenue side, US$210 billion is expected to be raised by imposing tax penalties of US$43 billion on people who do not have health insurance plans and another US$167 billion on employers that don't offer coverage to their workers

---

8   Kamarck, 2018.
9   Amadeo, 'How Does Obamacare Work for Me?', 2019.
10 Karavbrandeisky, 2010.

by 2025.¹¹ Another US$346 billion is expected to be raised from additional taxes levied on high-income earners.

Six years into its implementation, this programme had proven costlier than originally envisaged. The US budget deficit jumped to US $590 billion in the fiscal 2016, and US Government debt rose by US $1.4 trillion in the previous fiscal year. There was an additional expenditure of US$800 billion. According to an article by John Mauldin, the significant increased cost of insurance premiums for the 25 million people under the Affordable Care Act was not factored into the original CBO budget forecast. About US $75 billion of the additional US$800-billion spending was due to payments to Social Security, Medicare, Affordable Care Act recipients and others.

While Obamacare is noble and sound, the cost burden on the government has been substantial since its implementation. The financial and budgetary impacts of this act will flow into the decades to come.

The current Trump administration has ramped up its attack on the Affordable Care Act since entering office. In December 2018, a federal judge in Texas ruled Obamacare unconstitutional. While Obamacare is still standing, another six million Americans are expected to sign up in 2019.

Impressive Firsts and Records

Southeast Asia created its own significant history in this decade. In May 2018, Malaysia held its 14th general election (GE) and an unimaginable outcome was achieved. Former Prime Minister Tun, Dr Mahathir Mohamad, who formed a new coalition party, Pakatan Harapan, won the election and became the oldest serving prime minister on record at an advanced age of 92.

Emperor Akihito of Japan abdicated his throne on 30 April 2019, which makes him the first Japanese emperor to do so in over two centuries and marks the end of the Heisei period. He is succeeded by

---

11 Egstark, 'How is Obamacare paid for?', *Money 101*, http://money.com/money/collection-post/4537027/how-is-obamacare-paid-for/.

Crown Prince Naruhito. The 248th era has arrived and is officially named Reiwa, a combination of *Rei* – auspicious or good and *wa* – peace or harmony.

Thailand witnessed its own imperial transition, with the demise of its beloved king, His Majesty King Bhumibol Adulyadej the Great, to King Maha Vajiralongkorn in 2016.

Technology Companies Win

There were no technology companies listed among the world's largest companies in 2009. Seven were resource based. Royal Dutch Shell ranked at the top followed by Exxon Mobil in second position and Walmart in third. BP, Chevron, Total, Conoco Philips, Toyota Motor, Sinopec, and ING Group completed the list.[12]

A decade later, the list could not have been more different, with technology companies revealed as the new titans of industry. The largest company in the world in 2018 was Apple, with market capitalisation of US $926.9 billion. Apple was once valued at a trillion dollars. Amazon occupied the number 2 position with market capitalisation of US$777.8 billion. Other technology giants in the top 10 were Alphabet, Microsoft, Facebook, Alibaba, and Tencent. Berkshire Hataway Inc, Johnson & Johnson, and JP Morgan Chase represented the non-technology companies[13] on the list. Amazon and Microsoft have overtaken Apple at different times since 2018. How the world has changed in one decade.

Digital *Connections* and the Next Industrial Revolution

Industry 4.0 is touted as the next industrial revolution with its debut in 2010. This era rode on the invention of the Internet in 1993 and is known as the decade of the white-water world (WWW) in reference to kayakers navigating their kayaks in very turbulent and

---

12 'Global 500, 2009: Annual ranking of the world biggest companies', https://money.cnn.com>magazines>2009.
13 World's largest companies in 2019.

rapid waters, focusing on keeping a fine balance to get to safety. Volatile, uncertain, complex, and ambiguous (VUCA) are four nouns commonly used to describe the world we live in today.

Since the 1980s, personal and mainstream computing has progressed significantly, although the invention of computers occurred much earlier. We live in a world of mobile devices and wearables. The Internet of things (IoT) will further dominate every aspect of our lives and social media in the years to come.

Commerce in the digital- and applied-technology decade saw a trend in online trade and payment gateways. Physical stores are making way for digital ones, cash is becoming a currency of the past, and physical mail has been almost totally replaced by digital mail and the list goes on. We are more digitally connected than ever before.

Sharing Economy: A New Reality

Traffic congestion is not a new problem and governments around the world have been tackling it through various initiatives to control the number of cars on the roads. Schemes such as car-pooling, the odd- and even-number plate system, and weekday and weekend registration plates have been tried. Smart devices, good Internet coverage, and algorithms utilising advanced technology capabilities such as Global Positioning System (GPS) have enabled a sharing economy. The ability to match asynchronous demand and asynchronous supply in real time has revolutionised the transportation industry. The deployment through companies like Grab, Uber, and others, leveraging various technology platforms, has disrupted this industry. The fundamental concept of sharing has been extended to many other industry sectors including hospitality and sets the scene for other forms of economy that may come in the future.

Greed, Subprime Mortgage, and the Housing Crisis

While the pervasiveness of technology due to easy geographic reach and the speed of impact brought about by the power of the digital age was evidenced around the world in terms of the impact on businesses and the evolution of society, another mega storm was brewing – the *sub-prime mortgage*. Borrowers who would not normally qualify for conventional mortgages due to poor credit scores were able to obtain subprime mortgages with interest rates above the prime lending rate. This added fuel to the demand for housing. The US housing market boomed and peaked around 2003/2004.

Like any housing boom, there were a lot of speculative investments leading to an imminent bubble that can burst when fundamental economic factors change, such as a drop in housing demand, increased interest rates, or a rise in unemployment. When the economy slowed in 2006, many of these mortgages became distressed loans, causing a ripple effect on the ability of many banks and investment funds to survive. Some had to declare bankruptcy, and this severely damaged the US economy, leading to the subprime mortgage crisis in 2016, where over 10 million homeowners lost their homes. It also triggered the start of a significant financial crisis worldwide. In this period, the cost of housing fell and interest rates were raised by the Federal Reserve. Adjustable-rate mortgages followed the rate from the federal funds, which were later reset. The resulting high mortgage payments made it impossible for home owners to sell their property as the valuation was lower than their outstanding mortgage debt. This left them with no option but to accept foreclosure. The government could not do anything to save them.

Not all was bad news. Mr Maha Sinnathamby, a Malaysian immigrant credited with the development of Greater Springfield on the outskirts of Brisbane, was featured in a news article in 2017 for his bold move some 25 years earlier in real estate.[14] He saw potential in Brisbane in 1992, when he stood on top of a hill and looked across some 2,860 hectares of land that many considered too difficult to sell as it was covered with rocks. However, he saw the potential. More than two decades later, the land, bought with a business partner for

---

14 , Johnathan Pearlman, 'He came, he saw, empty bushland, he built a city', *The Strait Times*, 2017.

A$8 million, had turned into Australia's first private city known as Greater Springfield. According to Pearlman, A$12 billion has now been invested and it is already home to 32,000 people and has the capacity to grow to accommodate 200,000.

Slow Learners from Financial Crises

We are slow learners when dealing with crisis. There have been many forms of financial crises over the decades. Some notable ones in recent times include the stock market crash in 1973–1974, the Asian financial crisis (1997–1998), and the global financial crisis[4] in 2007–2008. In a globalised and *flat* environment, these crises instantly impact multiple countries, causing international financial concerns and further crises.

This decade has had its fair share of financial crises, notably the European debt crisis in 2010, where several sovereign states such as Portugal, Greece, Ireland, Cyprus, and Spain were unable to refinance government debt or bail out over-indebted banks under their national supervision bodies. They had to turn to international or third parties like the International Monetary Fund (IMF) for assistance. Other financial crises in this decade include the Russian financial crisis (2014) and the Greek Government-debt crisis (2010–2018). The Turkish currency and debt crisis, which began in 2018, is still ongoing and is characterised by the significant devaluation of the Turkish currency, high inflation, excessive borrowing costs, and the corresponding loan defaults. The high current account deficit and foreign currency debt are also contributing factors to this crisis.

Each time a crisis happens, policy makers, regulators, and governments will promise to prevent such failures in the future. The problem we see is that these crises still occur and the speed and pervasiveness, in terms of global impact and scale, has increased. We are indeed slow learners.

Stock Market Crash and Global Financial Crisis

There was significant business optimism and growth in 2007, and the market was riding high. In fact, the Dow hit its pre-recession high and closed at 14,164.43 on 9 October 2007.[15] This positive situation changed quickly.

The events that followed in 2008 clearly exposed the vulnerabilities of financial firms whose business models depended too heavily on uninterrupted access to secured financial markets at excessively high leverage levels.[16] On 15 September 2008, Lehman Brothers[17] filed for bankruptcy with US$639 billion in assets and US$619 billion in debt.[18]

The domino bricks fell one after another. The stock market, which had been bullish just 12 months prior, crashed on 29 September 2008. The Dow Jones Industrial Average fell 777.68 points in intra-day trading. Until 2018, it had remained the largest point drop in history. It plummeted because Congress rejected the bank bailout bill. But the stresses that led to the crash had been building for a long time.[19] By 5 March 2009, the index had dropped more than 50% to 6,594.44. Although it wasn't the greatest percentage decline in history, it was vicious. The 2008 crash wiped 50% off the index in only 18 months.

An article entitled 'Stock Market Crash of 2008' documents the chronology of the events leading to this Great Recession as depicted in my domino bricks illustration.

Table 2.1 is an abstract of the events leading to the stock market crash of 2008. As is seen in the table, the situation was clearly unstable with days of difficulty followed by days of improvements before sliding

---

15 Kimberly Amadeo, 'Stock Market Crash of 2008', 2018, https://www.thebalance.com/stock-market-crash-of-2008-3305535.
16 'Risk Management Lessons from the Global Banking Crisis of 2008', Senior Supervisors Group, 2009, Senior Publishers Group.
17 'Lehman Brothers Bankrupt', https://www.investopedia.com/articles/economics/09/lehman-brothers-collapse.asp.
18 https://www.sec.gov/news/press/2009/report102109.pdf.
19 Kimberly Amadeo, 'Stock Market Crash of 2008', 2018, https://www.thebalance.com/stock-market-crash-of-2008-3305535.

again. The events on the week of 15 September were happening on a daily basis and illustrate the now famous stock market crash of 2008. The stock market finally recovered in 2013.

Table 2.1 Abstract of chronology of events associated with the stock market crash of 2008

Year	Day	Month	Event
2006	17	November	The commerce department warned that October's new home permits were 28% lower than the year before. But economists didn't think the housing slowdown would affect the rest of the economy. In fact, they were relieved that the overheated real estate market appeared to be returning to normal. But falling home prices triggered defaults on subprime mortgages.
2007		August	The Federal Reserve (Fed) recognised that banks didn't have enough liquidity to function.
2008	End	January	At the end of January, the Bureau of Economic Analysis (BEA) revised its fourth-quarter GDP growth estimate down. It said growth was only 0.6%. The economy lost 17,000 jobs, the first time since 2004. The Dow shrugged off the news and hovered between 12,000 and 13,000 until March.
	17	March	The Federal Reserve intervened to save the failing investment bank, Bear Stearns. The Dow dropped to an intra-day low of 11,650.44 but seemed to recover. In fact, many thought the Bear Stearns rescue would avoid a bear market.
		May	The Dow rose above 13,000. It seemed the worst was over.

		July	The crisis threatened government-sponsored agencies Fannie Mae and Freddie Mac. They required a government bailout. The Treasury Department guaranteed $25 billion in their loans and bought shares in both agencies. The Federal Housing Authority guaranteed $300 billion in new loans.
	15	July	The Dow fell to 10,962.54. It rebounded and remained above 11,000 for the rest of the summer.
	15 (Mon)	September	The month started with chilling news. Lehman Brothers declared bankruptcy. The Dow dropped 504.48 points
	16	September	The Fed announced it was bailing out insurance giant, American International Group Inc. It made an $85 billion *loan* in return for 79.9% equity, effectively taking ownership. AIG had run out of cash. It was scrambling to pay off credit default swaps it had issued against now-failing mortgage-backed securities.
	17	September	The money market funds lost $144 billion. This is where most businesses park their overnight cash. Companies panicked, switching to even safer treasury notes. They did this because Libor rates were high. Banks had driven-up rates because they were afraid to lend to each other. The Dow fell 449.36 points.
	18	September	The markets rebounded 400 points. Investors learned about a new bank bailout package.
	19 (Fri)	September	The Dow ended the week at 11,388.44. It was only slightly below its Monday open of 11,416.37. The Fed established the Asset-Backed Commercial Paper Money Market Mutual Fund Liquidity Facility. It loaned $122.8 billion to banks to buy commercial paper from money market funds. The Fed's announcement confirmed that credit markets were partially frozen and in panic mode.

	20	September	Secretary Paulson and Federal Reserve Chair Ben Bernanke sent the bank bailout bill to Congress. The Dow bounced around 11,000 until September 29, when the senate voted against the bailout bill. The Dow fell 777.68 points, the most in any single day in history. Global markets also panicked.
	Early	October	Congress finally passed the bailout bill but the damage had already been done. The labour department reported that the economy had lost a whopping 159,000 jobs in the prior month.
	6	October	The Dow dropped 800 points, closing below 10,000 for the first time since 2004.
		November	The labour department reported that the economy had lost a staggering 240,000 jobs in October. The AIG bailout grew to $150 billion. Treasury announced it was using part of the $700 billion bailouts to buy preferred stocks in the nation's banks. The *big-three* automakers asked for a federal bailout.
	20	November	The Dow had plummeted to 7,552.29, a new low. But the stock market crash of 2008 was not over yet.
		December	The Fed dropped the Fed funds rate to zero, its lowest level in history. The Dow ended the year at a sickening 8,776.39, down almost 34% for the year.
2009	2	January	The Dow climbed to 9,034.69. Investors believed the new Obama administration could tackle the recession with his team of economic advisers. But the bad economic news continued.
	5	March	The Dow plummeted to its bottom of 6,594.44.
			Soon afterwards, Obama's economic stimulus plan instilled the confidence needed to stop the panic.

	24	July	The Dow reached a higher high. It closed at 9,093.24, beating its January high. For most, the stock market crash of 2008 was over.
2012	1	June	They panicked over a poor May jobs report and the eurozone debt crisis. The Dow dropped 275 points. The 10-year benchmark treasury yield dropped to 1.443 during intra-day trading. This was the lowest rate in more than 200 years. It signalled that the confidence that evaporated during 2008 had not quite returned to Wall Street.
2013			The stock market finally recovered. In the first six months, it gained more points than in any year on record. Stock prices rose faster than earnings, creating an asset bubble. The Dow set over 250 closing records until February 2018. Fears of inflation and higher interest rates almost sent the Dow into a correction. Like many other past stock market crashes, it did not lead to a recession.

A decade later, three key players Bernanke, Paulson and Geithner, who witnessed and managed various parts of this 2008 storm, came together and co-authored *Firefighting: The Financial Crisis and Its Lessons*. Ben Bernanke is an American economist at the Brookings Institution who served two terms as chair of the Federal Reserve, the central bank of the United States, from 2006 to 2014. Merritt 'Hank' Paulson Jr. is an American banker who served as the 74th Secretary of the treasury. Timothy Franz Geithner is a former American central banker who served as the 75th United States secretary of the treasury under President Barack Obama. The publication cited three proposals.[20]

The first proposal points out that imposing higher capital requirements on banks caused much credit creation to migrate to

---

20 Ben Bernanke, Hank Paulson, and Tim Geithner, 'Revisiting the 2008 financial crisis', *The Guardian*, 2019, https://www.theguardian.com/business/2019/may/29/bernanke-paulson-and-geithner-revisiting-the-2008-financial-crisis.

the non-bank sector, where US authorities still lack authority to intervene. They argue for an FDIC-style insurance model for the broader financial system.

Second, they note that the US system of financial regulation has barely been reformed despite the many weaknesses revealed by the crisis. In their view, 'the balkanised financial regulatory system could use reform, to reduce turf battles among redundant agencies with overlapping responsibilities.' Even after the Dodd-Frank overhaul, they lament, 'There is no single regulator responsible for safeguarding the system as a whole.' That is a damning commentary on the Financial Stability Oversight Council, which was supposed to fulfil that function.

The third proposal is targeted principally at the Trump administration, although Congress is again also implicated. Bernanke, Geithner, and Paulson believe that current US fiscal policy is deeply misguided. The deficit is too high at a time when the economy is growing healthily. That is bad economics today, and more importantly, the authorities could find it difficult to relax fiscal policy to combat a future recession. There is an urgent need to 'restock the emergency arsenal', particularly when there is relatively little scope to relax monetary policy. The Fed began a process of normalising monetary policy but has not completed the job, and President Donald Trump is doing what he can to prevent them from doing so by heckling from the sideline.

A Lost Decade for Americans – Poor Income Recovery for Middle America

The speed of recovery from the 2008 global financial crisis was unusually slow and was symptomatic of a permanent decline in GDP following the financial crisis since the economy never fully rebounds from the initial recession.[21] Estimates of long-term output losses ranged from none in Germany to almost 20% in Italy

---

21 Lydia Gordon, 'The recovery from the Global Financial Crisis of 2008: Missing in Action, 2014, Euromonitor International.

and Spain.[22] One related factor in the growth slowdown in more recent years is a growing ageing population, which is an economic social issue in itself. The decline in the growth rate of the working population (ages 15–64) can account for a decline of 0.7% in GDP growth rate in some advanced economies.

A decade after the start of the Great Recession in 2008, middle-class incomes are only just catching up.[23] Lehman Brothers collapsed in 2007 and many of the banks that were bailed out in 2008 rebounded long ago and went on to rake in greater riches. By contrast, many ordinary Americans are only now recouping their losses. The tightening of the labour market did not result in a rise in wages. Cassidy, quoting Trudi J. Renwick, a senior official at the Census Bureau, said that the 2017 median household income is not statistically different from the pre-recession estimate for 2007, thereby coining the phrase, 'middle-income Americans lost a decade'. Non-rich Americans bore the costs of the Great Recession and its lengthy aftermath. It was no wonder that they voted Trump into presidency with his promise of Make America Great Again.

Final Remarks for This Decade

In a blink of an eye, ten years have passed. Comparing my experiences of the previous ten years and those of the present ten years, the pace of life is certainly a lot faster. Work is done anytime and anywhere, enabled by digital mobile devices.

In the decade to come, we may see an adjustment in work policies to restrict time spent on mobile devices. This has already started to happen in Europe, where regulations are restricting work communication to within working hours only. There is also a consumer move to *dumb* phones over smartphones to restrict access to the Internet and limit communication to phone and text messaging.

---

22 Ibid.
23 Ten years after the start of the Great Recession, middle-class incomes are only just catching up, see, John Cassidy, *The New Yorker*, 2018.

A decade ago, the phrases *fake news* and *hashtag* were not common. Today, they are pervasive and various governments have passed laws on fake news. Privacy, civil liberty, and freedom of expression are hotly debated as part of the proposed laws with some convinced that the move to clamp down on social media's *fake* news is really an attempt to repress the public voice. We live in a volatile, ambiguous, and uncertain environment more so now than ever before.

The fight among the superpowers warmed up at the end of this decade. Trump's call to ban Chinese mobile phone manufacturers Huawei and Oppo threatens their business profitability and viability. Huawei is announcing its own operating system. China retaliated to the ban with a fine on US motor giant Ford in a move that is widely considered tit for tat. Huawei has been granted a limited role in developing the UK's 5G network, against the advice of Trump. Hindsight will reveal how this tech war plays out.

Does this mean a bleak future for us? I do not think so. It does mean, however, that we have to adapt to changes around us and be more mindful of what is ahead so that we stay ahead.

3.0

More Personalisation in a Hyper-Connected Decade

#A New Dawn

Understanding the future requires studying today's foresights, learning from past hindsight, and reflecting on today's insights . . . However, it is important to look ahead to stay ahead.

This chapter is about preparing for the future. The New Decade of 2020 has commenced with significant challenges. Record-breaking temperatures and months of severe droughts fuelled a series of massive bushfires across Australia. In addition, a Coronavirus disease (COVID-19), which is an infectious disease caused by a new deadly virus at the end of 2019 has subsequently become a global pandemic. This virus and its impacts have dominated global headlines daily. While this is happening, global trends that are changing the way we work, play and live continues. It requires a review of the trends and paradigms that are already in play today and imagining what is to come in the days ahead. Studying today's foresights, learning from past hindsight, and reflecting on today's insights make this an arduous and challenging task. Writing this chapter has proven to be far more difficult than the previous. Whatever is written here could be proven totally inaccurate in years to come or partially right or wrong at best. It is not written with the magic of a crystal ball, and therefore, I am certain it will not be totally accurate.

At the heart of human desire is the ambition to do well. There may be people who are cynical or disillusioned, probably because of past experiences. But most hope for a better future. Breakthroughs in science promise that one can custom co-design a baby with a doctor to one's choice and desires through genetic engineering by 2045.[24] There are many unsettling data and privacy issues alongside moral and ethical conduct to consider in all these possibilities. Science, however, is forging ahead and consumers will be given such options in the future.

With this in mind, this chapter is framed to help you think through some of these probabilities and possibilities and in so doing, prepare you for the probable manifestations of these trends and developments. Sudden, unexpected disasters and events that scar memories and mar historical records will continue to happen. At the time of writing this chapter, Taiwan reported a strong magnitude 6.1 earthquake on 18 April 2019 that affected Taiwan's coastal city of Hualien and impacted Japan and the Philippines. No one expected the fire that devoured the roof of 14th-century Notre Dame cathedral, one of France's most iconic sites.

We continue to live in an uncertain world marked by terrorist attacks. Peaceful New Zealand was shocked by the lone gunman who opened fire in a Christchurch mosque, killing 50 people and injuring 50 more on 16 March 2019.[25] What was more alarming was the fact that he filmed the entire crime and live-streamed it on Facebook. There was another report of violence where blasts at Sri Lanka hotels and churches killed 156 people on Easter Sunday the same year.[26]

It is often said that failing to plan amounts to planning to fail. Yet no amount of planning can mitigate some of the disasters mentioned

---

24 Jamie Metzl, 'Making babies in the Year 2045', *The Sunday Times*, 2019.
25 Jane Wakefield, 'Christchurch shootings: Social Media races to stop attack footage', *Technology*. BBC, 2019.
26 'Blasts at Sri Lanka hotels and churches kill 156" *AFP News*, 2019.

above, other than precautions and preparations to deal with them when they occur. My hope is that looking back on the 2020 decade in ten years' time will reveal a better decade where we have worked out how to manage risk more intelligently by pre-empting some of these possible occurrences and the precautionary steps taken to mitigate them.

What May Happen in this Decade?

Thanks to the Internet, it is relatively easy to scan major happenings and events scheduled in the coming decade. Society and human progress will be marked by the completion of iconic projects that will involve expenditure of billions of dollars, which in many cases spur domestic economies and help GDP growth.

China is already a world superpower and is on track to contend US as the biggest world economy. China's tenuous relationship with existing superpowers means it has yet to find its order. ASEAN aspires to be the fourth largest world economy by 2030. It is, therefore, expected that there will be some disruptions that may include the destabilisation of the Asia-Pacific region by American power. The current trade war between China and the United States has impacted companies' supply chain considerations as to the future locations of factories, treasury implications due to currency valuation fluctuations and overall lower GDP growth forecasts of many countries. Work force disruptions will be witnessed with the ongoing developments in future of work, future of mobility, and the future of X. The noun X here is a catch-all of many domains. Business transformation with focus on sustainable growth. Increasing profitability simultaneously is on many management agendas. Nuclear energy may be phased out in Germany while Turkey will be celebrating 100 years of independence in this coming decade. Block chain will be at a tipping point. There will be bioterrorism threats and higher unemployment due to robotic automation. Viewpoints on career have to be reshaped.

The business world will continue its massive makeover of the past ten years into the next decade. The way businesses and customers interact with each other has taken a different turn. A lot of this shift is because of business model changes and adaptations brought about by rapid technological changes and how cash as a medium for trade has changed. The journey towards *digitalisation* is here to stay and will accelerate in the coming decades. Co-working spaces have sprung up everywhere. Integrated food outlets, retail shopping, exercise fitness centres, and medical outlets are common features in new office blocks, the phenomenon of online shopping has exploded, and mobile devices have destroyed communication between humans at a dinner table.

Where to from here? There are trends that will be important in the 2020 decade.

Business (Un)usual, Breakthroughs, and More Transformation

This new decade can yet be another one of business as usual for most of the population. However, we may also face *business unusual* due to the disruptive forces of the technology revolution expected to drive the winds of change more aggressively in all sectors of society. The decade can be smoother by being more prepared or one can flow with the winds of change.

Governments responding to and driving this transformative change work through the ministries of finance, defence, science, education, and others. If there is to be a new ministry to drive technological integration, it should be named the ministry of futures and integration. This ministry would work across all ministries and drive integration across segments and sectors because disruption touches all sectors. Flexibility, agility, adoption, and quick response are key winning characteristics to determine success in the future.

From *Connections* to *Interconnectedness*

The Internet has been rapidly adopted and companies like Facebook, Amazon, and Google were quickly rushing to control the online space. Since then, SEO (search engine optimisation), social bookmarking, social networking, and other online activities that generate digital traffic have come of age.

The blog sphere, auto-responder email lists, and affiliate programmes all came out as good avenues for business reach and marketing to the masses. Online businesses have earned billions in profit conducting business through the Internet.

To cope with this increased load on networks, 5G technology[27] and architecture are expected to be the next evolution of the Long-Term Evolution (LTE) strategy of the mobile communications standard. In 4G, data speeds are up to ten times faster than the 3G network. Fifth generation (5G) is aiming to reach both high speed (1Gbps), low power and low latency (1ms or less) to cater to the needs of massive IoT, the tactile Internet and robotics.

Huawei, a young 32-year-old company founded by Ren Zhengfei in 1987 with a $5,600 investment, is today the world's largest telecoms equipment company with $107 billion in revenue and with customers in 170 countries in 2018.[28] Besides being a cutting-edge smartphone designer and manufacturer, it is touted to be the vanguard of 5G revolutionary technology that will fuel the driverless cars and smart factories of the Fourth Industrial Revolution.[29]

However, Huawei has attracted controversy and is under intense scrutiny after the United States told allies not to use the company's technology because of fears that it could be a vehicle for Chinese espionage. Huawei has consistently denied this.

Connecting the Unconnected

A rocket carrying six satellites built by Airbus Defence and Space and partner OneWeb was launched successfully in February 2019. The plan is to use the interconnected network of hundreds of satellites to beam high-speed, uninterrupted Internet signals to underserved

---

27 'Technology at its Best', https://www.specialevents.com/blog/five-top-technology-trends-increase-wow-factor.
28 Charlie Campbell, 'Leveraging 5G', *Time*, vol 193, no 16–17, 2019.
29 Campbell, p 100.

and unserved parts of the world by the end of the next decade.[30] This is the era of space Internet and OneWeb is one of its key pioneers.

The project aims to connect an estimated 650-strong satellite constellation in low Earth's orbit to provide high-speed, low-latency Internet services to areas that are beyond the reach of fibre-optic cables.[31] People in rural, remote locales and users outside the reach of terrestrial broadband coverage, including ships, planes, and emergency response services will benefit. As mentioned previously, science, space and satellites are dominating the coming decade's agenda.

By 2021, commercial services from OneWeb are slated to provide broadband capacity of one terabit per second and space, the Internet, and 5G are key infrastructure enablers of the digital decade.

A New Definition of Retail

The typical retail high street experience needs to be redefined. The shopping belts of Orchard Road in Singapore and many other cities worldwide are facing high rentals, expensive renovations, and lack of sales in-store. Forward-thinking retailers are experimenting with the concept and experience stores combining the physical and digital experience. The key is owning the loyalty of the customer. Customisation of the experience comes of age with the use of data analytics in segmenting and profiling the customer. Conversations are now being had around creating a new experience on the high street to bring communities together as traditional stores enter administration; unable to compete with online shopping alternatives and the high street, as it was, is increasingly turning into a ghost town.

---

30 'Connecting the Unconnected, AskStart', Science Section, *The Straits Times*, 27 April 2019, Singapore.
31 Ibid.

Cryptocurrency Becomes Understood and Accepted

David Chaum's digi-cash project looked promising but crashed towards the year 2000, and the business was rendered bankrupt. Several[32] attempts have been made to revamp the effort. One of the most successful of these was PayPal, the standard electronic transaction. Bitcoin, innovated by Satoshi Nakamoto in 2008, started the cryptocurrency revolution and the creation of online crypto currency exchanges. Despite being an unofficial form of currency, cryptocurrency has been accepted as a valid form of currency by many businesses, even in the physical retail space.

The Good, Bad, and Ugly of Globalisation

Amanda Huan and I co-wrote an article on the future of globalisation published by the Singapore Institute of Directors. We held the view that globalisation was once heralded as the beacon of hope for developing countries, an escape route that would allow them to climb out of poverty. However, an anti-globalisation backlash, tinged with the resurgence of nationalism, has put globalisation on the backseat. The swing of votes to far-right parties in Germany and other European states, Brexit, and the election of US President Donald Trump has reset the globalisation agenda.

Is My Dream Home Still Possible?

Speaking to any soon-to-be-married couple will eventually lead to discussion on the topic of housing and its reducing affordability. Next is the discussion on immigration policies, which have impacted employment and raised house prices. Politicians and government officials can no longer ignore this issue. Many measures to cool the property market and control speculative investments, unmanaged lending, and the housing bubble crisis have been introduced and legislated.

---

32 'Guide to understanding', https://medium.com/coinmonks/the-ultimate-guide-to-understanding-cryptocurrency-and-how-it-works-should-you-be-a-part-of-it/.

Not all economies have the housing affordability issues that plague Hong Kong, Singapore, and Australia in the Asia-Pacific region. I was quite shocked while taking part in a casual discussion with Japanese colleagues over dinner. I discovered that most people in Japan take the perspective that land holds value while buildings depreciate as soon as they are built. They would rather rent, although some do believe in owning their own home.

Smart Nation Singapore is described as 'Singapore taking full advantage of IT to transform into an outstanding city in which to live, work and play.'[33] It has set a target of 2025 to achieve this ambition. Singapore enjoys a high-quality digital network with high connectivity.

Affordable housing is one of the top political issues for the UK government. Britain needs about 30,000 new homes, and the supply is short of the requirement. Schemes like 'build to rent' are one of the options. The concept of co-working and co-living within the same complex is gaining popularity as an alternative way of thinking about home ownership paradigms.

In Singapore, investors and non-Singaporeans have to pay more to acquire and sell properties. This is also the experience of property investment in Australia. Lending is at an all-time low. Elsewhere the picture around the world is similar. National and local perspectives on rising entry prices have made owning a home very difficult for most families and the high rates in interest are not making it any easier.

Housing schemes differ by country, but the intention is to help the younger population own a home.

Integrity and the Ethical Economy

Fake news, gender diversity, equality, anti-harassment laws, proactive actions, hashtags, Me Too, and various other campaigns are common signs of the times. Stock exchanges, regulators, and

---

33 Dana Van der Zee, 'Smart Nation Singapore', 2017, Holland Innovation Network, Netherlands.

stakeholders are calling for transparency and higher accountability on management actions. Employee conduct is tracked, monitored, and reported. Ethics hotlines encouraging whistle blowing are on the increase.

We are increasingly seeing mission statements of organisations focusing on value, ethical behaviour, and integrity. From the sharing economy we see today, I believe the agenda for the decade to come includes the ethical or trust economy.

Bite-Sized and Timely Learning for Deep Skills

The Singapore government's vision is for Singaporeans to adopt lifelong learning. It is recognised that conventional education models are out of date. Continuous learning has to be adopted for the workforce to be relevant and timely. Vocational training is also important. In Singapore, agencies like Skillsfuture are set up to address the implementation of the recommendations. Digitalisation is creating new industries as well as transforming many existing ones, such as finance, advanced manufacturing, and healthcare. It further spells out that digitalisation will give businesses, big and small, an effective means of reaching global markets.[34]

The Smart Nation vision to be delivered by 2025 needs to tap on the economic opportunities offered by the digital economy. Adoption of digital technologies across all sectors of the economy is a necessary requirement. In addition, strong capabilities in digital technologies must be built, in particular, data analytics and cybersecurity, which can be applied flexibly across sectors. Data will be an increasingly important source of comparative advantage, and we need to improve our ability to use it productively in the economy. Learning curricula and pedagogy will have to be aligned with this strategic change in order to achieve this requirement.

---

34 'Report of the Committee on the Future Economy', CFE, Singapore, 2017.

Ageing Well

All countries in Asia and the Pacific region are ageing at an unprecedented pace. Statistics in 2016 indicated that 12.4% of the region's population was 60 years old or older, but this is projected to increase to more than a quarter (25%) or 1.3 billion people by 2050.[35] By that time, Asia Pacific is expected to have 59% of the world's population over 80 years of age, about 152 million people compared to 53% at present.

This has serious implications on the provision of appropriate healthcare and long-term care, as well as income security. Domestic expenditure on healthcare support for the ageing will increase. Healthcare systems are expected to be redesigned to cope with population growth and value-based wellness-healthcare expectations. The study recommended more initiatives to encourage intergenerational interaction, such as housing nurseries and eldercare facilities within a common development.

The demographic transition towards an ageing society in the Asia-Pacific region has critical social, economic and political consequences. Governments are actively working on programmes to leverage international frameworks.

The Dragon on the Throne: China Becomes the World's Largest Economy

It was declared in 2015 that China was now the world's largest economy, which shifted the power of economic balance, making the European Union the second- and the United States of America the third largest economy. The US debt held by China is about $1.13 trillion[36] in US treasuries. In August 2007, there were threats by China

---

35 'Ageing in Asia and the Pacific: Overview', United Nations ESCAP, Bangkok, 2017.
36 'U.S. Debt to China', https://www.thebalance.com/u-s-debt-to-china-how-much-does-it-own-3306355

to sell a section of their holdings if there was continued pressure to increase the value of the yuan.

According to Standard Chartered economists, the long-term growth forecasts are underpinned by one key principle: countries' share of world GDP should eventually converge with their share of the world's population, driven by the convergence of per-capita GDP between advanced and emerging economies.[37]

Are We Ready for this Decade?

As I stated at the beginning of this chapter, the above are loose predictions of what possible challenges face us in the decade ahead and what the consequences might be. Only time will reveal the truth. Yet we must consider the possibilities so that we are as prepared as we can be, learning from the past as we try to interpret the future. In the following chapters, we will look at ways to aid that preparation.

---

37 United States will drop to become the world's third largest economy behind China and India by 2030, new financial rankings suggested by Ariel, Zilber, 2019.

Sharing Lives

4.0
Amazing ACE

#The Pioneer of Patient-Centric, Research-Led Health Care

For Dr Lim Cheok Peng, a career practising medicine was not in the cards. A desire to improve the delivery of healthcare rose as a greater passion. He achieved that vision as chairman at China Medical & HealthCare Group Ltd, managing director and director at IHH Healthcare Bhd, president and chief executive officer at Parkway Group Healthcare Pte Ltd, and executive vice chairman and managing director at Parkway Holdings Ltd. In these capacities, he led his teams to pioneer patient-centric, research-led healthcare. It is a role he accepted initially without any business or management experience. However, in true entrepreneurial spirit, he went with the flow and ended up building a healthcare empire and legacy that will benefit patients in the Southeast Asia region for generations to come.

From Humble Beginnings

Born in Ayer Itam, Georgetown, Penang, in 1946, Cheok Peng Lim was raised in Penang in the post-war years, as one of two brothers and three sisters. His father was a merchant trading between Indonesia and Malaysia but was forced to retire early in 1963 when his business was destroyed due to the unrest – Konfrontasi – between the two countries during Sukarno's presidency.

While his parents funded his brother's studies as an architect, it was his grandmother, his greatest influence as he was growing up, who stepped in to pay for Cheok Peng's medical education when his father's business failed. Dr Lim also attributes his entrepreneurial bent to his grandmother, who ran a hotel and provision shop. He could sit for hours as a child listening to her wisdom. She lived long enough to see him graduate as a doctor.

His sisters also excelled in their own careers, having been educated in the UK or Australia. One was a ballerina. Another was a pianist and violinist who now teaches music in Sydney, Australia. The other studied as a microbiologist but didn't practise, instead turning her focus to running a home for abandoned babies for a Kuala Lumpur charity.

From the Practice of Healthcare to the Business of Healthcare

Dr Lim studied medicine at University of Singapore and returned to Malaysia to complete his compulsory residency as a doctor before starting his private practice as a GP. He became increasingly frustrated by the failure of the state to provide adequate medical care in the region and realised that private medical facilities were the solution. So he opened a private polyclinic in Kuantan which thrived, and eventually, as one of a community of doctors, he established a private hospital in the same town.

Notwithstanding this success, Dr Lim did not stay on to see the hospital develop but instead decided to resume his training as a cardiologist in London in 1980 and furthered his studies in San Francisco from 1983 to 1984. Having his children disrupted his education, and he returned to Singapore in 1986 to set up a permanent home for them.

He found a position with Mount Elizabeth Hospital at a pivotal time in Singapore's economic growth. However, when Gleneagles Hospital was mooted for sale in 1987, Dr Lim's friend, property developer Tony Tan, made him a proposition, 'I buy but you must run it.' The property was bought under the Parkway name and Dr Lim found himself running the facility with no prior business knowledge. While he'd founded the earlier hospital in Kuantan, he hadn't stayed around to acquire any experience running it. Nevertheless, his vision was to transform Gleneagles Hospital into a state-of-the-art medical facility to rival Mount Elizabeth Hospital, which was being developed with some major international investment at the time.

'We knew the hospital had to be different. It had to be run and administered by the doctors,' recalled Dr Lim. 'Who but a doctor would be around at 3am in the morning or be able to recognise the needs of staff or identify gaps in the system?' His style of management worked. He was a people person who wasn't afraid to get involved and listen to the staff on the ground, jumping on problems immediately and solving them.

Parkway soon gained the reputation as a specialist hub, and in 1995 the opportunity came to buy Mount Elizabeth Hospital. With the deal, Parkway Holdings became one of the largest private healthcare providers in Southeast Asia, comprising 17 marketing offices around the region including in Brunei, Vietnam, India, and Middle East and more than 60 medical centres, clinics, and ancillary healthcare businesses as part of the IHH Group. Understanding the importance of educating nurses, he established Parkway College in 2008 with aspirations for it to be a global leader in healthcare and professional education.

Dr Lim was keen to achieve an enduring sense of accord within the organisation and a sense of *family* spirit among staff. He was known to be good natured and an excellent delegator, trusting his team to manage tasks alone but there to lend help or advice if needed. With a clear succession plan in place, Dr Lim handed over the helm in 2015 having left an enviable legacy in healthcare not just in Singapore but around the region.

The Passion That Drove an Honourable Entrepreneurial Career

For Dr Lim, patient care was more than simply treating the patient. While he started as any other doctor, trained in medicine to practise and treat patients in a patient-centric setting, it wasn't long before he found his passion in investigation and diagnosis.

Over the last 40–50 years of his working life, he has found satisfaction in discovering new things, in curing patients of illnesses as a result of new developments in medical research and enhanced medical facilities designed around the patient.

There have been many accomplishments. Instead of being in the practice of healthcare, he has found himself in the business of healthcare, building hospitals and clinical research institutions. He was a pioneer in setting up centres of excellence within hospitals – a novel concept at the time.

'General hospitals get all sorts of things right. But unfortunately, knowledge and value creation are not there as you are a generalist not a specialist. So, setting up such specialist centres within the hospitals was a pioneering approach.'

Not a Journey Taken Solo

Dr Lim is humble in his accomplishments and knows he could not have succeeded in his vision alone. Building the right teams of course had a part to play, but Dr Lim points closer still to home for his driving force. 'Without the ongoing support of my wife, there is no way I could have accomplished what I have,' he says. 'She has been by my side over 40 years. She looked after the kids in the early years as I pursued my qualifications and earned a living. She is absolutely paramount to my success.'

The couple has been married for 47 years and have three daughters and one son, all of whom have become doctors and specialists.

A Family Man at Heart

For Dr Lim, his family is everything – the centre of his world and it is on them that he spends extravagantly. 'Our children all live with us with their families. All expenses are paid by me and my wife. That includes their meals, travel, and provision of home help. Our mansion is large enough to accommodate a family in each wing, so they have their own separate homes, but within the family compound, so we all remain close. When we go out to eat as a large family, the bill is always on us. That's our extravagance. It works for our family and it's a pleasure to keep the family happy.'

Dr Lim has properties abroad that have been bought as an investment for his family and part of his legacy. These include holiday homes and apartments. 'We don't rent these out. They are left empty so that anyone in the family can stay there on holiday at any time of their choosing,' Dr Lim explains. 'This is the Lim dynasty.'

Philanthropic Mission

In retirement, Dr Lim divides his time between his grandchildren, church services, charity work, and his other passion, cooking. He cooks Penang comfort food for his family on a daily basis. His charity work revolves around education, just as his medical work did.

'Every path to success starts with education. It is so crucial to set one up in life and is the key to leading countries out of poverty. This is my new focus today,' Dr Lim explains. 'I'm involved in charities that work to educate child migrants and displaced refugees. We are looking at how to educate them for a good start in life. Without that, they can't go far.

'We are funding e-learning initiatives to support their education.'

Rethinking Training for a Better Quality of Care

Looking ahead, Dr Lim understands that education is key to delivering a quality healthcare system. Part of this educational focus is on nurses. Parkway Nursing School in Singapore trains nurses from overseas. This is so important given the challenge in the local labour market in attracting people into the nursing profession. Gleneagles Nursing School in Kuala Lumpur, Malaysia, trains nurses for Malaysia's own consumption.

'We are doing things differently than in the past,' Dr Lim explains. 'To assure quality of care, nurses need not only the theory but the practical hands-on training. This didn't happen in the past, but we are committed now to ensuring that our nurses spend more than 50% of their time in practical training. They can acquire the knowledge as they practise. They need to be exposed to real patients and real medical cases. This must be done, however inconvenient it may seem administratively.'

Dr Lim acknowledges that management needs to balance quality of training with the need to deliver for shareholders. 'We still need to operate as a profit centre, but we also need to manage investor expectations. Healthcare is not an overnight success. You need to be prepared to invest for the long term. We are talking around eight to ten years. Just as education requires patience, so does investing in healthcare. Investors need to exercise patience. We need to focus on the patient and then there will be financial profit in the long term.'

One of the ways that Dr Lim envisions healthcare to be a success is to train more mature candidates, who he recognises as making better doctors. Dr Lim also notes that grade A students don't necessarily make good doctors. It's one thing to have the IQ or intellectual skills to learn the theory of medicine. But the key to great patient care, and the making of a good doctor, lies in EQ or emotional quotient – their bedside manner – the ability to empathise with and listen to the patient and then propose the best care for that individual.

'We can't compare the care of the past with that of today. We are living in different times. But we need to analyse and address why quality of care fluctuates. What is the legacy we leave behind?'

Dr Lim has been thinking about that legacy. Looking 20 years into the future, he sees three large gaps in care that need to be plugged:

1. *Quality of care.* It's unfortunate that standards of care have dropped. We see a lot more complaints and patients aren't getting the service they need as compared to what we see from admissions records previously. We really need to address this.
2. *Cost of delivery.* The governments of every developed country have acknowledged that medical costs have gotten out of control, and it's a matter that preoccupies me. How do we package good, affordable healthcare? Superior care is no longer affordable. You just have to look at cancer treatments today. These are simply not affordable.
3. *Education.* As I've already stated, we also need to examine where we position ourselves in terms of education. I repeat this because it is so critical to the future of healthcare. How do we train doctors and nurses and transition that training away from the classroom and into the wards? How do we evolve this and think differently?

Planting the Seeds for Change

Dr Lim acknowledges accomplishments in setting up various educational facilities aimed at addressing the current healthcare delivery shortfalls. Associated medical university in Kuala Lumpur is one success. Dr Lim sees this experiment as not a bad idea. But will the focus be on teaching or research? This is yet to be seen.

'We also need to consider the kinds of doctors we are churning out. It is not enough just to get the numbers up by churning out doctors in volume. Are we producing the type of doctor that will help patients and will this attempt ultimately result in good affordable healthcare?' he questions.

Another promising development is Khazanah's IMU, which is advancing the quality of clinical training. 'We need to continue to attract top universities as partners and create win-win opportunities here. Otherwise our doctors will train abroad and likely remain there. If we hadn't created these opportunities here, Singapore would be in dire straits today.'

IMU is the only medical university in the world that makes a profit. Dr Lim warns that we need to continue to evolve and restructure. IMU is now more than 20 years old. 'We need to take stock. We are at a crossroads, a crucial next chapter. Are we going to be a big batch university with our own degree and our own teaching hospital, and do we do the training elsewhere?'

Singapore is small so Dr Lim sees the next wave of growth in Malaysia, Vietnam, Cambodia, Turkey, China, and the Middle East. Having built the foundations in Singapore, he is now happy to take a back seat and see where the gaps are. 'There is still a lot of work to do. There are gaps I mentioned that we need to fill, and this is where we are today.'

No Regrets

Asked if he had any regrets, Dr Lim only wonders how life would have transpired if he had trained more and worked as a fully fledged cardiologist instead of taking his entrepreneurial route.

'On hindsight, my career divergence has been worth it,' says Dr Lim. 'I was looked down on by some as a wheeler dealer. Building commercial businesses is not something a doctor should do. Maybe they are right, but ultimately that was my calling, and I am proud of all I have achieved. I am able to be proud because I have always acted with a conscience. I've never cut corners to make a fast buck. I got my values from my grandmother and the way she brought us up, and I'll always be grateful for that upbringing and to her. She always taught me that it was OK to make money as long as you act ethically. For me now, that means not to cheat the patients.'

Passing Good Values down to the Next

Now in the golden years of his life, and with a wealth of life and business experience behind him, Dr Lim feels obligated to pass forward some key learnings to the next generation.

Not every person is intellectually clever. We all have different skills and different parts to play. Just as my role wasn't to practise medicine but to build medical businesses to serve in a greater way, so we all have our paths in life. But whatever path one chooses, one will always do well following the five tenets I have lived my life by:

1. *Before you can give advice, evaluate the person's character.* People have different strengths, characters, and exposures to life. You need to consider their world view and experience as well as their character and personality type and give advice to them in the best way they can take on that advice. You need to assess people for the roles they are capable of taking on. If the role calls for a safe pair of hands, you don't want to put a risk taker who doesn't consider consequences in that role. Are people employed in the right roles to help the patient? The number one consideration in anything we do is – don't harm the patient.
2. *Be ethical.* Have integrity in whatever job or occupation you choose. This is so important. Don't do things just for the money. You need to have a passion for what you do, otherwise don't do it. Don't chase money. It will come to you if you deserve it. Above all, don't cheat people. Blessings will come to you when you follow the right path.
3. *Do what you know best.* Focus on what you can do well. Become an expert in one niche rather than trying to be a generalist in all things. Do not try to do what you are not trained in. You can't be a master in everything. You are only waiting for a disaster if you put untrained people in a role.
4. *Look after your family.* Your family is your most important treasure. Love them, look after them, and put them first. They are, after all, what you are working for.
5. *Pray to God.* He gave you life and will always look after you. He will not fail you.

Reflections

ACES Criteria	Reflections
Do they fulfil dreams and passions?	
Do they create or capture value as per life's mission?	
Can the values and benefits be shared for the greater good?	
Do others judge the achievements as great? (Wow, you aced this!)	
Will they create a better future – legacy?	

5.0
Sisters' Company

#Be the One – Lyddia Cheah
#Success after Comeback – Soniia Cheah

Not many people can claim they have achieved significant self-actualisation in their lives and have a world ranking to their names in their chosen fields. Well, the Malaysian Cheah sisters, both Lyddia and younger sibling Soniia, have achieved this feat.

Cheah Sisters' World Stage

The emotional thrill and adrenalin rush when the final shot seals the victory in any final match is always sweet.

'We're often physically exhausted and mentally drained, but the roaring and support from the crowd, the banging of the drums, the waving of the national flag make every effort on court worthwhile and help us savour more future victories' (Lyddia and Soniia).

This scene is what most world players are looking for when chasing success in tournaments. The harder they fight, the sweeter the feeling. It is equally important that professional players learn to handle defeat, loss, criticism, and sometimes seemingly *unfair* comments and move on to the next challenge. One has to be thick-skinned, meaning not be easily upset or insulted when facing criticism. These bitter and sweet life lessons have helped the Cheah sisters to be stronger over time and more determined to be at their best in their craft.

In the Cheah family, Lyddia and Soniia are two of the family's three daughters to have achieved international fame and clocked their respective highest world rankings of 29 and 23 in competitive badminton.

The Acts on This Stage

Their chosen act is competitive badminton. They are talented national players who represented Malaysia in many world and regional tournaments in their prime years. Younger sibling Soniia is still competing professionally and representing Malaysia in the women's singles category. Lyddia, however, has retired from the national squad and is now pursuing her Master's in Mechanical and Manufacturing Engineering in the United Kingdom. Having retired from the national squad to pursue her tertiary education, Lyddia subsequently played competitively again by joining AirAsia Badminton Academy as well as Team Derby in the UK, where she is studying.

Key Facts at a Glance

Name	Lyddia	Soniia
Chinese name	Yi Yu	Su Ya
Birth year	1989	1993
Ambition	World champion during competitive career era. Updated to educational excellence alongside continuing to develop as an athlete[1]	World champion
Highest ranking	29	23
Career titles	3	2

Height	177cm	175cm
Handedness	right	right
Career wins	139	137
Category	women singles (WS)	women singles (WS)

ACES

The Cheah sisters' list of achievements in badminton is long. They have conquered different junior, national, and international competitions throughout their careers, and their respective medal cupboards would fill many cabinets and make a proud display in the family home.

Lyddia

Lyddia gained prominence in the national badminton arena when, at 15 years of age, she became the youngest ever women's singles finalist in the National Grand Prix Finals.[38] She went on to help the Malaysian girls' team as a 16-year-old player to finish as the runner-up in the Asian Junior Championship for the first time in 2005. Her goal was to break through and join the national team, which she did. She subsequently flourished.

Lyddia achieved a gold medal in the mixed team event at the 2010 Commonwealth Games in New Delhi. Her other highlight was gold medallist in the women's team at the 2009 Southeast Asian Championship in Vientiane, Laos.

---

38   Teik Huat Lim, 'Third time lucky?', *The Star*, 13 May 2006.

Player of the match 2019 in Big BUCS Wednesday

2016 world junior championships, partner with Woon Khe Wei in the team event

Qualified for world chapionship 2015, when I was with the AirAsia badminton club

Soniia

In her earlier career, Soniia's accomplishments were just as impressive when she represented Malaysia at the 2009, 2010, and 2011 Asian Junior Championships and World Junior Championships in 2011 in the mixed team event. She participated in the 2010 Summer Youth Olympics as well as the 2011 Commonwealth Youth Games and, like her sister, also progressed to the national team.

Soniia achieved her first international title at the 2016 Belgian International tournament and was a silver medallist in the mixed team event at the 2018 Commonwealth Games. Her Southeast Asian Games record includes both silver in the 2017 women's singles and women's team events and bronze in the 2011 women's team event.

After winning the world number 6th He Bing Jiao.

The expression winning the world number 2 Akane Yamaguchi

Cheah United

There are examples of family dynasties in badminton. In the 1970s, we had Tan Aik Huang and Tan Aik Mong, brothers who represented Malaysia in the Thomas Cup, Southeast Asian Games, Commonwealth Games. and other Asian championships. The Sidek badminton family is also a legend. All five brothers were world-class players in the 1990s. and it was the Sidek brothers who invented the tricky S serve. Sisters Ng Hui Lin and Ng Hui Ern were national players in the 2010s. Hui Lin's highest ranking was 16 in 2009 and Hui Ern's was 20 in 2014 before they retired to pursue their careers.

If the Sideks were famous for their S *(Sidek) serve*, what about the Cheah sisters? Well, their trademark is their height. Both are known as the tallest female players in Malaysia. Their height advantage helps them deliver sharper slices and smashes, which makes them formidable opponents.

The Cheah household, particularly the parents, must be very proud of their children Lyddia and Soniia. Theirs is a tremendous story of sacrifice and complete dedication to their goals and aims in life. Achieving success in terms of the ultimate pinnacle of one's dreams at such an early age is satisfying. What's more, if navigated correctly, the path ahead can be even more glorious.

A common factor seen in the stories of these aces is the strong support received from the immediate family. In the case of the Cheahs, their father is a banker and their mother is in business, and the couple is always present when needed to support their daughters. Their mother will of course be worried about injuries, and their father is there to be the pillar of strength, providing whatever support is needed for them.

The sisters enjoy a cordial and respectful sibling relationship. In some ways, it is unique in that they were competitors on occasion since both of them were in the national team. Yet they have achieved a strong bond with each other. The youngest, Juliaa, heads the family fan club for the sisters, although she herself has not taken the same path into badminton. And according to Lyddia, as a teenager, Soniia would look to her older sister for trends from anything from taekwondo and badminton to fashion and hairstyles. As the expression goes, the Cheah sisters are said to be of the *same mould* and therefore, the pair strongly supports one another. As they have moved on with their professional lives, this has always been a great source of support and comfort for each of them. The family is tight knit with father and mother being the bedrock.

We are stay as one

She's my inspiration for who am I now.

We always support each other. My Pillar of strength.

Mastery at the Highest Level

Sports on the international competitive stage is highly intensive. It involves strategy and the technical execution of shots that requires great hand-eye coordination, skill, precision, agility, and an ability to rapidly read the game before a near 500kph smash comes straight at you. Split-second reflexes are required throughout the matches. Feedback from several former international, world-class players point to strategy in court and aligning the tactical play during the matches. All players are competent when they reach this stage in their careers.

Derek Wong, former Singapore's number 1, points out that players in the top 20 category are more or less the same in terms of speed, stamina, agility, and strength. He further comments that the only factor that can help minimise the long rallies is when you have many special shots or great skill to manoeuvre the opponent to create an opening to go for a killing shot. The skills of the top 5 world players are at another level.

Lyddia and Soniia know this well and their day-in and day-out trainings are to hone their skills at the highest level. This is a given and there are other factors at play in the ecosystem that are worth mentioning. These are outlined the Rubik's cube of sports below.

Commonwealth Games 2010

Continue my passion with Team Derby

Won the match against former Olympic champion Li Xue Rui.

The ACE Rubik's Cube of Sports

The pressure of world-class competition is intense. Climbing the ladder in the world rankings is one long journey and reigning in the circuit is another. This is why grand masters like Lee Chong

Wei are respected legends. He held the world number 1 ranking for 349 weeks (over six years) including a 199-week streak from August 2008 to June 2012.

Chaos to Pattern is the core theme for attempting to solve a Rubik's cube, the puzzle which has fascinated millions of people across the world. The permutations and combinations of turning the many faces of the cube is likened to the many factors that have to line up to make one successful in badminton. The 9 (3x3) factors are:

1. physical-mental-emotional health
2. technology
3. learnings from the master
4. knowing the enemy and knowing yourself
5. the power of having fun
6. the magic of a break and reflections
7. the jersey, the bag, and the walk down the corridor into the court
8. dealing with PMT (prematch tension)
9. defeating the enemy

1. Physical-mental-emotional health

A competitive sports player requires strong physical, mental, and emotional health. Their entire life centres around training, competing in competitions, and, regardless of the outcome, repeating the cycle again. Competitive sport is demanding on the body. Besides skill and mental resilience, strategically responding on court makes the difference between winning and losing. There are good and bad days in competitions, and dealing with the emotions of bad judgement, inaccuracy, and errors only serves to increase the mental pressure. How the four elements of physical fitness, mental strength, emotional management, and superior skills combine in each player determines their success.

2. Technology

Today, technology is an additional element in the success formula. The playing pattern and speed in badminton has changed over the years. This is because of technological advancements. New materials and design result in lighter and more powerful racquets. The material used on the court surface has provided a better grip, which in turn has resulted in improved safety for the players. New cushions used in the shoes provide better protection on the ankles and increased comfort for the feet. A better, consistent quality of shuttlecock is a result of improved aerodynamic design. Clothing designs have also benefited from technological advancements. And Hawk-Eye's SMART Replay technology is used by many of the Badminton World Federation (BWF) tournaments to help officiate on a number of infringements including line calls and service faults.

Dietitians, experts on food, nutrition and health, play an important role in designing and customising diets for athletes, supported by insights analytics. As people have become more aware of wellness and live more active lifestyles, sports medicine has become a growing business. In treating sports-related injuries and overseeing rehabilitation, doctors now use technology-enabled medical devices.

Viewers enjoy real-time broadcasts on matches and tournaments throughout the world. They are part of the action without having to be physically present at the arena. As such, players have access to videos to study and analyse their opponents' play at the click of a button. Lastly and most importantly, coaches are a key part of the athletes' lives. They are constantly by their side, giving tips and moral support. They too use technology to keep track of their athletes' progress and enhance their coaching techniques when working with each individual in improving the consistency of their winning mentality and game.

3. Learning from the master

Dato Lee Chong Wei is a national hero and badminton legend. He is the Cheah sisters' senior and a mirror to learn from. Prior to his retirement, the sisters got to participate in the same tournaments most of the time from 2017. They learnt a lot from him in the tournaments, both inside and outside of training sessions.

They learnt that, for a professional athlete, mental preparation and discipline in everything they do are very important. They have to be aware of their own body condition and adjust and prepare for matches. They know that their eating habits have an effect on body health. The right supplements taken daily help the joints and muscles to recover faster.

It is fortunate that their training time coincided with that of Chong Wei's and that they got to train with him on occasions. One sentence sums up what they have learned from him: 'Never say I'm done.' Therefore, they will always give more than 100% in their training and push themselves beyond their limits.

Interview session with media after training.

4. Knowing the enemy and knowing yourself

'If you know the enemy and know yourself, you need not fear the result of a hundred battles. If you know yourself but not the enemy, for every victory gained you will also suffer a defeat. If you know neither the enemy nor yourself, you will succumb in every battle' (Sun Tzu, *The Art of War*).

To the avid follower of Sun Tzu's strategies, it is this message – to observe and to draw conclusions based upon knowledge of the environment – that allows the strategist a tangible, quantitative advantage over their opponents. Good strategy fits nicely between environment (including the opponent) and the player. It is, therefore, incumbent upon the player to learn how the competitive ecosystem really works, observing fresh situations in that light, not being prejudiced, and making conclusions based upon the facts available. To succeed and sustain, one must observe, learn, reflect and fine-tune continuously.

The coach plays a crucial role in helping the player win the competition and at the same time know the opponent's strengths and weaknesses well so that a strategy to win can be designed and trained, either to overcome the limitations or take advantage of the opponent through the player's unique capability.

Lyddia and Soniia list their top 3 enemies on the court:

Enemy A: Mindset

A more experienced player has a greater level of confidence than a younger player. Discouragement and self-doubt resulting in lack of focus and confidence can result in a loss.

Enemy B: Fatigue and focus

Routine can be boring. Yet it is fundamental to training on-demand responses through reflections on action. Fatigue of the body can be a challenge. Overcoming fatigue and burn out is key to sustainability for every athlete.

'At match time, focus throughout the game is everything. One has to overcome a tendency for lapses in concentration,' Lyddia explained. She added, 'I have the strokes and I am ready for the challenge. It is just that sometimes I tend to give away points when I am leading. I have to avoid this.'

Enemy C: Skill and leveraging one's competencies

Coach Choong Hann commented that Soniia cooperates well and works hard to tackle problems. However, there is still much ground to cover, such as on-court training to get her into better shape and off-court training to strengthen and condition her.[39]

5. The power of having fun

Lyddia agrees with former Badminton Association Malaysia (BAM) technical director Morten Frost, who was a world-class player himself, 'I believe you need to enjoy what you are doing. Passion is the leading key to success.'

However, her passion for badminton slowly faded because the day-in, day-out training in the national squad had become a routine, and she felt greatly discouraged due to non-performance even after training hard. She felt like she wasn't making headway in her career. This faded passion resulted in her not enjoying the training anymore, which was one of the reasons she left the national team. When she went to the UK to pursue her education, she resumed her training and regained her passion and started competing again.

---

39 'It's time for Soniia to step up', *Daily Express*, 14 May 2019, www.dailyexpress.com.my>news.

Always love the difference if my "off-court" outlook.

My favourite place to have a holiday is staying in a resort with nice beach

University of Derby Sport Awards 2018, sport team of the year

Graduation 2018, Soniia had to stay back for training.

6. The magic of a break and reflections

Pursuing her studies in a new environment gave Lyddia a fresh perspective on matters. Before, she had doubts in her ability and questioned why she was unable to perform after training so hard and why there was so much opposition. Her frustrations were compounded by self-doubt that spiralled downwards to lower self-worth with thoughts like not being a good player and not having achieved anything.

However, when she started to reflect on why she took up badminton as a career in the first place and the lessons she had gained along the way, she realised that there was always something to learn from every training session and every match, and that was an achievement in itself. She learnt to embrace herself more, knowing that it was not an easy journey to reach where she is now and to be proud of her achievements.

The upward spiral kicked in. She began to enjoy the game more because it was a process of learning each time, and she appreciated each chance on the court. With this came a clearer vision in her mind as to what and how it should be done.

Another perspective she realised was that she must be realistic and progressive. As the Chinese saying goes, '一山还有一山高 (*Yī shān hái yǒuyī shāngāo*)', meaning there is not a mountain which is the tallest. Younger players with better skills and stronger physical strength will appear in the competitive arena, and we must move on and progress with new life goals and objectives.

7. The jersey, the bag, and the walk down the corridor into the court

According to the Cheah sisters, who are familiar with the mixed emotions felt during the long walk to the court, they described the feeling as complicated. They sometimes feel excited, sometimes nervous, and at times really comfortable and happy to go on court. The feeling that comes up at any given match depends on which competitor they are playing and their current physical condition. They are also aware of how much their mental condition influences the outcome, for what one thinks determines how one plays. Badminton is always a mental game and the strongest opponent is not the person standing on the other side of the net but rather, one's own mind.

8. Dealing with PMT (prematch tension)

It is normal to have prematch tension, no matter how well one is prepared. However, one can turn it into motivation and excitement by telling oneself to be confident and enjoy the match. The tension is always there when the mental priority is on winning and losing. A way to reduce the tension is to focus on the process, like what should be done. Let the outcome be the judge and let winning and losing merely be part of the game.

9. Defeating the enemies (both internal and opponents)

The last component is injury, which is the biggest enemy for any sportsperson. A distinctive hallmark of the Cheah sisters is their characteristic aptitude of 'no matter what'. This has become evident having researched both the sisters' competitive journeys over the years.

Soniia's Injuries and Comeback

Soniia ruptured her Achilles tendon in August 2013 and was on crutches for four months. The wound was infected after the first surgery, and she had to undergo four further surgeries just to remove the infection.[40] There was a deep and open wound, and she had to visit the hospital daily to get it cleaned. She could not rest her right foot on the floor or sleep at night because of the throbbing pain.[41] She was traumatised. She was even afraid to step into the training hall for fear of aggravating her injury. Looking back on it now, she thought she was going to lose her mind.

It took almost three years before Soniia was fully fit to return to the competitive circuit. She endured many rehabilitation and therapy sessions during that time, and just a year after her injury,

---

40 'Injuries', *Badminton Planet*, 18 September 2017.
41 Rajes Paul, 'Sonia's back training after horrible year of injury', 12 September 2014, www.thestar.com.my>sport.

she attempted to return to competition, but it was too early. Her recovery was incomplete. She found the pain, the waiting process, the idle downtime, the not being able to compete, and the therapy sessions very frustrating. By the time she returned to competitive sport, her rankings in the BWF World Rankings had dropped from 34 all the way to 422.[42]

While it was the most challenging time of her life, Soniia was quick to add that she learned many valuable lessons during the down period. She discovered who her friends in name were and who her true friends were. Some were well-meaning but were unable to help her, and some were those that could have helped her but were not around in her time of need. There were those who paid lip service and frankly did not bother. Some were even callous in their remarks. Learning this lesson to discern intentions and true friendship as a 20-year-old is a good thing.

The comeback was significant. Her world ranking has jumped to 23, and she is ranked number 1 in Malaysia. Now ranked 183 globally, she won her first international title at the Belgian International Challenge Badminton Championship in Leuven, Belgium, in 2016.[43] This was three years after her injury. She then went on to capture her first national title in the women's singles category of the Celcom Axiata National Championship in 2018. 'Finally, I've won my first national title. It means a lot, especially after coming back from a career-threatening injury,' said Soniia. The objective ranking of 34 (pre-injury), 422 (lowest), 183 (recovery), and 23 (peak) is in itself a demonstration of comeback victory.

---

42 'Soniia happy to put injury nightmare behind her', www.stadiumastro.com>artikel.
43 Vincent Liew, 'Soniia Cheah overcomes career threatening injury to win first title', 18 September 2016, www.badmintonplanet.com.4592.

First time walking on sand afer several times of surgery for my Achilles' tendon unjury.

Never stop training during holiday.

Lyddia's Injuries and Comeback

Lyddia certainly empathises with Soniia's feelings. She too had her fair share of injuries as a sportsperson.

Her tenacity in her craft was demonstrated way back when she was a 16-year-old junior competitor attending the Kedah Open tournament in 2006. A motorcyclist knocked her down while she was crossing the road as she was returning to her hotel. She suffered head and leg injuries but still played in the open. She remembers that she was not able to concentrate due to her injuries but played on anyway.[44] This is a true demonstration of 'no matter what!'

Four years later, injuries suffered by both Lyddia and teammate Julia Wong threatened to wreck Malaysia's hopes of a breakthrough in the Uber Cup Finals in 2010. She sustained the injury during training.[45] The resiliency was seen in her determination despite the injuries. She was a gold medallist in the mixed team event at the 2010

---

44 Teik Huat Lim, 'Third time lucky?', The Star, 13 May 2006,
45 'Injuries to Lydia, Julia put semis target in jeopardy', *The Star Malaysia*, 28 April 2010, www.pressreader.com.

Commonwealth Games. A year prior, she won the bronze medal at the Southeast Asian Games in the women's singles event in 2009. She lived up to expectations and won the Maybank Malaysia International Challenge tournament when she overpowered Singaporean seventh seed Liang Xiayu in 2012.

Prepare for the Next Act

The key is always to look ahead. Martin Luther King Jr once said that human progress is neither automatic nor inevitable. Every step towards the goal of justice requires sacrifice, suffering and struggle; the tireless exertions, and passionate concern of dedicated individuals. It is evident that both Lyddia and Soniia live out this principle in their lives.

Lyddia: Contemplations

Lyddia's injuries dashed her hopes for the 2013 World Championship. It was the same year that Soniia injured herself. Lyddia decided to retire from the world of competitive badminton she had been part of for 11 years and resumed her studies.[46] At her announcement, she explained, 'I have decided to stop because of a combination of reasons, but the main one is because I want to further my studies. I started my A-Levels three years ago but took a break because of badminton . . . I have no regrets because I know I've given my best. My junior days were most memorable because I did well in the Asian and World Junior Championships.' Both sisters are thankful that they had the best of support from their parents during 2013, a tough year for the Cheah sisters.

---

46   Rajes Pau, 'Lydia calls it quit after 11 years', 25 July 2013, www.thestar.com.my>sport.

Lyddia: Resume or Come Back

After quitting the badminton national team, Lyddia continued her passion in badminton with the AirAsia Badminton Academy (AABA) in 2014 while studying. After her A-Levels, she went on to complete a degree in Mechanical Engineering and is currently completing her Master's degree in Mechanical and Manufacturing Engineering at the University of Derby, where she joined Team Derby to participate in England's National Badminton League.

Career tiles include runner-up at the Bulgarian International tournament in the women's singles and doubles events. In 2017, Lyddia won the Iceland International tournament in the women's doubles event and was runner-up in the singles event. In addition, she was bronze medallist in both World University Games 2015 and 2017, and represented her university, winning several medals in the British Universities and Colleges Sport (BUCS).

Lyddia: Next Act

Lyddia personally believes that success is balancing work with passion, learning something new each day and more importantly being happy and grateful. Establishing a set of goals for her professional and personal life is important to achieve the success that she believes in, developing a personal strategy comprising all the essential and distinctive things that help to keep performance at the highest level.

For example, one of her strategy plans is *Understanding myself with the help of intellectual things*. She takes a couple of minutes each night to record some key learnings from the day, as learning something new each day is one of her definitions of success. Then she takes 1–2 days at the end of the year to reflect on the year and brainstorm several personal and professional goals for the upcoming year.

By doing this, she has a clearer vision of what she wants to pursue in the new year. Sometimes she may lose focus on what she needs to achieve throughout the year, so an annual review of goals helps her stay focused on what she is passionate about.

Soniia's Contemplations: The Journey to 2020 Tokyo Olympics

Steve Jobs used to advocate DREAM BIG. Soniia's dream is to become a world champion, and she is single-minded in chasing this dream.

She is embracing the challenge of being the sole candidate in the battle for a place at the 2020 Tokyo Olympics. Instead of being weighed down by the task, she considers it a privilege to carry on the nation's fight for a ticket to the badminton competition in Tokyo.

Love to travel and experience different culture. See how big is the world

Doing the Right Thing and Doing It Right

The sisters' individual purpose is clear. For Lyddia it's #Being the One and for Soniia it's #Success after comeback. Their ambitions and strategies to follow are laid out. It is, therefore, now about execution. They have displayed tremendous tenacity in their pursuits. Given their experience with the nine factors of success, they will continue to turn the Rubik's cube to align the component faces and achieve the success they have outlined for themselves.

In the words of Yik Xiang Loo, who was ex-backup team member of the national team, his coach advised him in four phrases. At all times in life:

- go all out
- never give up
- fight to the end
- never say die

I can see all elements at work in the Cheah sisters.

Reflections

ACES Criteria	Reflections
Do they fulfil dreams and passions?	
Do they create or capture value as per life's mission?	
Can the values and benefits be shared for the greater good?	
Do others judge the achievements as great? (Wow, you aced this!)	
Will they create a better future – legacy?	

6.0

Painting Your Own Rainbow

#Focus on Abilities

Noah Tan presenting his painting of President's Challenge Logo to President of Singapore, Halimah Yacob

Noah Tan Kai is an 18-year-old Singaporean teenager at the time of this book's publication. While most kids are enjoying their teenage years, and the boys are getting ready to enter national service, not many are able to boast of meeting presidents, prime ministers, VIPs, CEOs of major corporations and special brand ambassadors, or winning awards, contributing to society and being acknowledged for their talent and skills. The story of Noah Tan is inspiring. He is a special kid.

Diagnosed with autism spectrum disorder (ASD) at an early age, Noah has been introduced to many different activities, hobbies and events from a young age, his mother's way of ensuring that he integrates as much as possible with society. It became obvious early on that Noah had a passion and talent for painting, and over the years, he has garnered many awards for his craft and been showcased on important stages.

Noah's World Stage

There is a line in the song titled 'At the End' by Earl Grant that goes like this: 'At the end of a rainbow, you'll find a pot of gold.' The pot of gold may be akin to the recognition and awards Noah is now receiving as an artist. His scope is expanding beyond his current horizons and art. So too is his world stage. He is now also doing well in bowling (another passion), and badminton has just been added to his list of triumphs.

Noah and Art

'Painting makes me feel happy and relaxed' (Noah).

Art has certainly helped calm Noah and has provided him with an avenue to focus and develop his artistic skills. Noah is a student at Rainbow Centre, which runs schools and programmes for children with disabilities, and Noah was accepted into its Talent Art Programme for showing so much promise at painting.

Rainbow Centre Chair-ity Fundraising Noah doing a live painting with Mdm Ho Ching (Guest of Honour)

VSA & SG Cares Celebrating Our Culture of Love. Noah Tan working on his painting

Futuristic Singapore painting for SMRT at the New Chua Chu Kang Interchange by Very Special Arts Sg

PRISM – Rainbow Centre Fundraising Art Exhibition with Professor Tommy Koh (Guest of Honour)

One time, when I visited Rainbow Centre's art studio, he wrote, 'Cyan, Magenta, Yellow' on the board and introduced the colours to me. He loves his fluorescent colours. On the table was a picture of The Fullerton Hotel and his sketch of the hotel outline. He was getting ready to paint the next addition to his impressive portfolio.

His art has also been featured on more unconventional canvases including chairs and an EZ-Link card produced by Very Special Arts (VSA) Singapore. The tribute to Noah on the back of the card that features his art pretty much sums up this special artist: 'Playing with vibrant colours is Noah's strength as an artist. He has impeccable taste in matching hues and shades.'

As a VSA beneficiary, Noah was accepted and enrolled into the Visual Arts Certificate programme offered by the VSA and Nanyang Academy of Fine Arts (NAFA). According to Noah's mother, he enjoyed the programme very much, and it has helped further develop his skills as an artist. His work has been frequently included in many fund-raising charities by corporations including Woh Hup and Deloitte.

Among his outstanding awards include the MOE Lee Kuan Yew Exemplary Award, Rainbow Centre Margaret Drive School's Most Outstanding Award, and certificates of recognition in the Singapore Youth Festival (SYF) art exhibitions.

Following the successful charity event at Deloitte where we raised over S$20,000 for Rainbow Centre back in 2016, I was told that Noah enjoyed bowling. Since we have an ex-national bowler in my department, I arranged to gift Noah a bowling ball with his signature on it. Noah was definitely pleased with the gift. In return, I was surprised to receive a painted bowling pin from Noah. What a nice gesture from a young boy!

Noah with Dr Janson Yap of Deloitte SEA
Colours of the Future Fundraising event at
Deloitte SEA Awesome Residential

Noah, Bowling and Special Olympics Singapore (SOSG)

'Let me win, but if I cannot win, let me be brave in the attempt.' Noah recites the SO Singapore Athletes' Oath

The Special Olympics is a global inclusion movement using sport, health, education, and leadership programmes every day around the world to end discrimination against and empower people with intellectual disabilities. Founded in 1968, this movement has grown to over five million athletes and unified partners in more than

170 countries. It has the support of over one million coaches and volunteers.

Special Olympics Singapore (SOSG) was set up in April 1983 as an adjunct committee of the Movement for the Intellectually Disabled of Singapore (MINDS) and the Association for Educationally Sub-Normal Children, now renamed Association for Persons with Special Needs.

Noah joined SOSG at age 13 in 2013 in the pioneer batch of the Learn to Bowl Programme. He progressed fast and in 2014, came in second in the SOSG Bowling competition. In 2017, he represented Rainbow Centre Margaret Drive School (MDS) and won two golds, in both the singles and doubles categories in the SOSG National Games 2017. That same year, he won another gold at National Para Bowling 2017. He was also trained for the Special Olympics World Summer Games 2019 as a reserve but was unable to take part due to his commitments in the NAFA Visual Arts Course.

In 2019, Noah was part of the Rainbow Centre MDS team that won a gold in the National School Para Bowling Competition. In the Play Inclusive Badminton Competition by SOSG, SportCares and supported by MOE, he also clinched a bronze to add to his silver of the previous year.

Noah's Many Awards

Each podium moment is a special time for Noah and his family, and there have been many of them. Here, I highlight his most outstanding achievements just over the last five years.

	Competitions and Awards	Recent 5 years
1	VSA International Art Competition award	2014
2	VSA Singapore Annual Art Competition	3rd in 2016 and Consolation 2018
3	Special Olympics 9th National Games for Bowling	2017 (Gold, Single & Double)
4	Singapore National Para Bowling	2017 (Gold)
5	Rainbow Centre MDS Most Outstanding Student Award	2014, 2015, 2016, 2018
6	SYF Certificate of Recognition	2014, 2016, 2018
7	MOE Lee Kuan Yew Exemplary Student Award	2018
8	NAFA Certificate in Visual Arts – Distinction	2019
9	Inclusive Sports Badminton competition by Special Olympics / SportCares / MOE	2018 (silver, double) and 2019 (bronze, double)

| 10 | National Schools Para Bowling competition | 2019 (gold, single) |

Noah Gives Back

While receiving support from Rainbow Centre and other ecosystem support agencies, Noah has, over the years, been actively playing his part in contributing back to society with his participation and contributions.

	Fund-Raising Events and Achievements	Last 5 years
1	A Kaleidoscope of Colours: Murals at Novena Underpass – UOL and VSA	2014
2	S.E.N.D for Hope E Christmas Card - Capital Land x MDS and Community Chest	2015
3	Colours of Our Future: Fundraising Event at Amara Sanctuary Sentosa – Deloitte Singapore and Rainbow Centre	2016
4	Welcome to My World: Rainbow Charity Fundraising Showcase	2016
5	Woh Hup Appreciation Night Fundraising Event - VSA and Woh Hup	2017
6	*Colour Our World*, Noah's artwork on SBS Transit Bus 16 and Limited Edition – Pilot Pen 100 years Anniversary and Rainbow Centre	2018
7	Rainbow Center Charity Golf: Auction of Artworks	2018
8	VSA Limited Edition EZ-Link Card: Spring	2018
9	Futuristic City of Singapore Artwork at CCK New Bus Interchange – SMRT and VSA	2019
10	VSA NDP 2019 greeting card in the fun pack	2019
11	President's Challenge: Art in the City Singa Exhibition at Raffles City – VSA	2019
12	Futuristic City Artwork – Woh Hup and VSA	2019
13	Rainbow Center Art Exhibition: PRISM at The Fullerton	2019

14	ComChest Award: Live Art Painting at Istana – Rainbow Centre	2019
15	President's Star Charity Show – VSA	2019
16	Rainbow Centre Graduation Ceremony: Valedictory Speech by Noah	2019

Noah as a Barista

Rainbow Centre is committed to empowering its students to be able to integrate into society. At 18 years old, Noah will soon graduate from the school. At Seeds Café in its Margaret Drive campus, he is training to be a barista. His responsibilities include operating the coffee machine and doing latte art. The goal is to train him in a trade so that he has employable skills in the future.

Intern barista at Seeds Café Rainbow Centre

Noah's Rainbow

The first letters of each colour of the rainbow speak eloquently of Noah's attributes.

Colour	Positive attribute	Commentary
Violet	Victory over circumstances	Despite the limitation, he has overcome many earlier challenges.
Indigo	Intervention and industrious	Early intervention is key for addressing autism. Autistic kids are focused on what they do, and Noah is industrious.
Blue	Blue skies ahead	His favourite colour and his positive attitude.
Green	Go for Gold	His many achievements and topping the list.
Yellow	Yellow – colour for royalty	He has the favour of royalty, meeting heads of nations and governments.
Orange	Opportunities	Continuous open doors and opportunities.
Red	Ready and resourceful	Always getting ready for the next challenge. Grateful for the resourcefulness of the ecosystem support to meet the ongoing needs of special children.

Noah's Support System

Rainbow Centre – empowers and thrives for people with disability
Rainbow Centre is a non-profit organisation in Singapore that envisions a world where persons with disabilities are empowered and thrive in inclusive communities.

The organisation works with its partners to create opportunities for persons with disabilities to make the most of their abilities and participate meaningfully in society. Through practical education, meaningful support, and effective training programmes, Rainbow Centre strives to improve the quality of life for them and their families. Established in 1987, Rainbow Centre is a registered charity and an Institution of Public Character.

Such institutions have proved to be a very important vehicle in helping Noah and his family cope with his condition. Its person-centric approach, being a good listener to what the family defines as a good life, and support for them in their journey speaks well of the way Rainbow Centre operates. Their approach to co-create an inclusive community deserves the respect and applause of society.

Provider and Protector to Promoter

Noah's mother, Rosyniah Wang, is always present. She has been Noah's primary caregiver and protector since birth and now takes on the additional role as manager, in helping to promote Noah in all his activities. Rosyniah, known to her friends as Rosy, is of Peranakan descent. Prior to giving up her career to look after Noah, Rosy was a leading air stewardess, her first and only job. Her husband is the sole breadwinner in the family, and Noah's brother completes this family of four.

One of the character traits of ASD is a short attention span, and Noah was quite hyperactive in his early years, which made social life awkward. Today, Noah does not get distracted as much and can paint for many hours in one sitting, especially when he needs to complete his project. Initially, Rosy had to plan and write out his schedule and timetable. As he grows older, he can plan his time better on his own and things are lot easier for both mother and son as a result.

Rosy's Reflections

'He is different, but not less. Noah chooses to focus on his abilities, not his disability' (Rosy).

In Rosy's words, 'Noah was born in 2001 and diagnosed with ASD when he was two years old. When the psychologist at NUH (National University Hospital) told me his diagnosis, my mind just went blank. I teared up and a thousand questions flooded my mind, Why me? What have I done wrong? What is autism? How am I going to take care of a child with special needs? It took a while for it all to sink in.'

Dark Nights

'It was initially difficult to accept Noah's diagnosis. After I got over my denial, I started to seek out all possible cures for him, like trying out a programme started by a pioneer in the treatment of brain-injured children in the United States. I also considered bringing him to Kuala Lumpur for Neuro Acupuncture and Herbal Medicine treatment by a well-known Chinese physician. All of these treatments gave us hope for a cure at the time. We eventually came to accept that there is no cure for autism, but it can be better managed through early intervention and therapies.

'Initially, it was a lonely journey as all my friends and relatives did not have children with disabilities and found it difficult to understand my situation. Crying myself to sleep was the only way to release my daily stress and worries.

'Noah faced many challenges when he was a child. He was hyperactive, had high anxiety, and liked a set daily routine. He didn't start to speak until he was five, engaged in very little eye contact and kept very much to himself. Autism has impaired both his social and communication skills.

'When Noah was going through puberty at around 10–12 years old, this was the most stressful time for me. He melted down in public often and would scratch and bite me when he was upset. He liked to do things in patterns and routines, and I would have to accommodate. For example, although we have two lifts in our block, he would insist on taking the same one each time even if the other is available and empty, and when dining out, he would insist on sitting at the same table each time and would melt down if someone else was sitting at it when we arrived. One can imagine the awkwardness of these demands in public.

'I confided in his teachers at Rainbow Centre when I could no longer handle him alone and requested to see a school psychologist for help. Being a mother with a special-needs child means I have to make a lot of sacrifices, like not being able to do things that I used to do and having to turn down friends' invitations and gatherings. My life revolves around Noah. If you see Noah, you will see me. Without a helper since day one, I have had to oversee his daily routines and make sure he has social exposure like bringing him to school at Rainbow Centre MDS, art lessons at Very Special Arts Singapore, and Special Olympics Singapore bowling trainings.'

Birds Singing at Dawn

'Noah has come a long way. I am thankful to all his dedicated and patient teachers at Rainbow Centre, his art teachers at VSA, and his coaches at Special Olympics Singapore. It really takes a village to raise a special child like Noah. With motivation, exposure, and support, he can achieve his dreams. I hope that the public can accept people with autism like Noah. He is different but not less. As his mother, I will be his pillar of support and walk this special journey with him to achieve his dreams. He has taught me to see things from his unique perspectives. Noah chooses to focus on his abilities, not his disability.

'Noah's self-discipline and work ethic have definitely contributed to his achievements. Every day is an opportunity for us to journey together, no matter how tough it is.

'I am blessed to have Noah as he has taught me a lot of things in life, like patience, unconditional love, true happiness, and most importantly, faith. Without Noah, I believe I would not be the person I am right now.'

Learning from Noah

I first met Noah when I conducted a charity event for Rainbow Centre, and I learn something new from him each time I meet him. These lessons are just as applicable to anyone else.

Noah reminds me to:

- nurture a strong spirit and beliefs
- overcome obstacles
- stay hopeful for a better tomorrow
- pursue bite-sized learnings
- focus on the things at hand
- sense the environment, protect, and guide
- build a future.

Noah's Journey from Here – Barista or Noah's Art Gallery in the Making?

Rosy and Noah were busy preparing for a filming session when I met them to research the materials for this chapter. I could see that Rosy was very excited. Mediacorp was filming Noah for the President's Star Charity Show to be aired on TV on Channel 5. This is just one of many times Noah has been featured in the media.

But where does he go from here? The answer lies in his passions and abilities. Perhaps Noah can be both a barista and a renowned artist. His works are worthy of being showcased in his own art gallery, where he could display and sell his paintings. The ongoing exposure will allow him to accept commissioned work as he has been doing in Singapore and even beyond, where Noah could venture internationally.

With the Inclusiveness Agenda at the forefront of many organisations' value systems today, employers and employees are being encouraged to play their part in social impact programmes. Noah cannot do it alone. and the ecosystem must chip in to support and help him succeed in this journey.

Reflections

ACES Criteria	Reflections
Do they fulfil dreams and passions?	
Do they create or capture value as per life's mission?	
Can the values and benefits be shared for the greater good?	
Do others judge the achievements as great? (Wow, you aced this!)	
Will they create a better future – legacy?	

Noah's Album

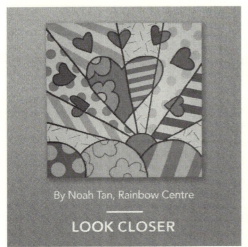

7.0

All It Takes Is the First Break

#Connections

Have you heard of the phrase, 'lucky break'? Many aspiring actors, singers, and musicians are looking for a lucky break in their careers. When they do become successful, they point to the one song or movie that gave them their breakthrough. 'All it takes is that first break' is a common observation of the rich and famous.

'With a guitar in my hand, I like to connect with people through my music and songs. My dream is to become an outstanding artist, sharing my songs and music worldwide. My genre is pop rock. I am Kent Tonscheck, a singer and songwriter from Australia.'

Looking for That First Break

All of us are in different stages of our business and career. Some have achieved success while others are content with their status quo. Some succeed in their dreams only to subsequently fail.

This story is about an up-and-coming artist in search of his lucky break. He has every reason to be confident and optimistic about his career. His profile and experiences are similar in many ways to those who have already found fame. His talent is promising. First, his voice is heavenly. Second, his lyrics, melody, and arrangement in song composition have matured over the years as he has plied his craft as a professional artist. Third, his journey includes the usual highs and lows that go with the profession, from the mountain-high experience of performing to a cheering crowd and the valley-low feelings of being down to your last few dollars. Most important of all is his passion for his craft and the *never-say-die* attitude that gives him the tenacity to overcome his challenges and to be ready to be successful.

In terms of relevance to this book, he co-wrote 'I am ready for MORE' with me, a song that is uploaded to YouTube and other digital platforms and is featured in a later chapter in this book. The sound engineer and producer of the recording studio was extremely complimentary of the song and Kent's golden voice.

Kent Tonscheck's Stage

Kent's stage is one of a farm boy working towards his dreams to becoming an international artist. Performances in local semi-rural Australia, cities, and international stages are the different acts he has played on his stage. Slowly and surely, the list of acts will grow, both in scale and quality.

Since his graduation from university, Kent has worked as a retail assistant, barista, and various other jobs while performing gigs in the evenings and on weekends. This journey to build his profile as an artist has taken nearly five years, and today, he is a full-time artist.

Songwriter and Singer

Kent's passion for music surfaced early. There is a photo of him playing the family piano when he was just 14 months old, probably his first taste of music. As he got older, the passion for music intensified, and in 2011, when he was still in high school, he got his first shot at fame, performing on Australian TV on Channel 10's *Creative Generation* programme. This was his first taste of performing before a large and appreciative audience. The experience was addictive and made him hungry for more. His decision to pursue music not just as a hobby, but as a career, was a departure from the family tradition, where all family members worked in the family farming business. Kent was the first in his immediate family to go to university and leave the farming business, and the only one in his extended family to be a performing artist professionally.

As testament to his immense musical talent, Kent's golden voice won him a runner-up solo vocalist award at ARTS (Applause Rising Talent Showcase) International in Florida in 2014, where he shone against an international group of musicians.

Kent was performing at his commencement when I spotted him. A friendship developed out of that encounter, and we have since written several songs together.

Better Now and Not Later: Mountain-Top and Valley-Low Experiences

#YOLO – *you only live once* is a common catchphrase among young people. The idea is to pursue one's dream while you are here. This level of perseverance and commitment can be viewed as stubbornness by some. For those who understand, it is simply about passion and having no alternative than to go for it.

Kent has lived through his share of mountain-high and valley-low experiences in pursuit of his dreams. The good news is that some of these low and dull experiences are now behind him. He counts his few episodes of performing in Singapore as mountain-top experiences. He is humbled and excited by the fact that someone living 6,150 kilometres away and who only knows him casually is willing to invest in his talent and support it vigorously. We recorded a few songs together in a Singapore recording studio. This experience invigorated his passion for travel and singing internationally. The next stop was the Philippines, which is known as the land of songs and singing. With such exposure, Kent is gearing up to live his ultimate dream – to play in packed stadiums around the world.

Most start-up artists lack opportunities and resources, and Kent is no different. When he first moved from his hometown of Toowoomba to Gold Coast in search of opportunities, everything went wrong. The job at a local cafe he thought he had was delayed, leaving him with no income. To make matters worse, his car broke down and finding money to pay the rent was a consistent battle. In those early days, he hadn't yet built up a network to fall back on. Friends were telling him to quit and find a *real* job and his bank balance was down to just a few dollars.

Forever Grateful

His low moments forced him to assess whether this was truly his life purpose and calling or whether he was just being selfish in wanting to have a career in music because he really enjoyed it. But he soon realised that he wasn't the only one enjoying it. He found that connecting with people on an emotional level through the international language of music brought complete strangers together in such an indescribable euphoria. When Kent saw how his music touched people, it made all the struggle worthwhile.

Knowing that pursuing his dreams was something he had to do, Kent got on his knees in prayer and reflection and put full trust in his creator to pull him through. He had to have faith that music was his doorway to show love to and positively impact the world he lived in. He had to believe that God would make a way. Sure enough, God prompted an extremely lovely lady from his church to give him a room to live in for free for a few weeks until he got back on his feet. The local cafe finally opened, and he could start to earn some income and save enough to rent a place with a friend who wanted to move to the coast as well.

He may have had no place of his own, no money, and had a broken-down car, but he never had a broken-down dream. He still stays true to his purpose and knows that when he makes that world tour, he will never forget where he came from and the people God sent into his life to get him there.

Love – the Maiden Song

The first experience, the first product is always special. 'Love' is the title of Kent's first release, and it is about that feeling one gets when one has experienced an unsuccessful relationship in the past and is constantly wrestling with self-evaluation and the question of how to make it better next time. 'Love, love, love, love, love, don't, don't, don't give up' is the chorus.

Love Life and Tales is the name of his EP. It features his songs 'Love', 'I'm Not Ready', and 'What Kills Me'. This debut EP is available on www.CDbaby.com and iTunes. Song by song, the collection is increasing, and the next goal is album 2.

Uniquely Aussie

Chris Hemsworth, best known for his role as the Nordic god of thunder Thor, is an Australian actor.[47] He has just wrapped up *Avengers: Endgame*, which is the highest-grossing film in history at USD2.79 billion in 13 weeks. This is his seventh outing over ten years in the Avengers franchise. The second of three sons of a social worker father and a teacher mother, he cut his teeth as an actor playing bit roles on Australian television prior to his breakthrough. This came when he landed a regular role as surfer Kim Hyde in the soap opera, *Far and Away* back in 2004.

Another Australian icon is the pop group the Bee Gees, formed in 1958. Their music is evergreen and still popular some 60 years later. But fame was not immediate for them either. Frustrated by their lack of success, the brothers returned to the country of their birth, England, in 1967, where they received news that their song 'Spicks and Specks' had been awarded Best Single of the Year by Go-Set. The Bee Gees had found their own breakthrough, that 'first breakthrough song' referred to above.

---

47   Poh Kim Wong, 'Chllax with a top bloke,' *The Straits Times*, 27 September 2019.

Other Aussie celebrities include Kylie Minogue, AC/DC, Mel Gibson, Olivia Newton-John, Keith Urban, Rick Springfield and the list goes on. Each had their struggles and has their own unique story.

Music in Australia: Better than Before

Australia is becoming really supportive of its musical artists from an industry point of view. There are government grants and scholarships to help artists develop professionally, and there are many very good music school programmes around the country. The issue I see is that people who go to festivals tend to go more for the atmosphere and big artists than to see a smaller band or potentially discover a new favourite artist.

I have heard of many independent artists who have flown themselves to Germany or Japan to play some self-promoted smaller shows. They print their own flyers and hand them out on the street in the day and play to a full venue at night. The people just love live music so much, they don't even need to know who the artist is to pay $15–$20 at the door and enjoy their night.

In Australia, the majority couldn't care if tickets are only $10. If they aren't a fan of the artist, or the artist is not that well known, they simply won't bother turning up. Every established artist was once an unknown, playing small venues to people who cared enough to go see them and invest in them before the hype. I wish more people cared enough to support live shows of all sizes.

Making It in Australia

How do you know if you've 'made it'? It really depends on the definition of success in one's mind. For some, it is enough to live in a van and play shows up and down the coast, meeting people and seeing different landscapes. They just have to promote themselves really well, be excellent communicators, and play their incredibly well-written songs, sell their merchandise, and keep writing new content. They are contented, happy, and successful in their own minds.

If one wants to make enough to live a dream lifestyle, such as having an extravagant house with a view, fast cars, and designer clothes, then these artists need to find deals that will get them incredible international reach. They have to work really hard to create excellent songs, play exciting shows, and enjoy the hustle and bustle of crowded places and high-pressure performances.

Either way, one has to be a hard worker, musically on top of one's game and always willing to learn and evolve with the industry.

#Wireless for Sound

The entertainment and music industry are examples of industries significantly disrupted by technology. Professor Clayton Christensen best summarised his earlier views on disruption in his book, *The Innovator's Dilemma*, back in 1997: 'First, disruptive products are simpler and cheaper; they generally promise lower margins, not greater profits. Second, disruptive technologies typically are first commercialised in emerging or insignificant markets. And third, leading firms' most profitable customers generally don't want, and indeed initially can't use, products based on disruptive technologies.'

We know the reality of disruption has progressed and disruptive products create a different value. It is not necessarily simpler and cheaper. The impacts of the disruptions are worldwide. Think of what Alibaba has achieved. Leading firms want to copy and use these examples as icons to emulate.

US Recorded Music Revenues (in $billions)

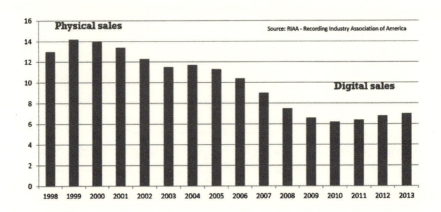

US Recorded Music Shipments (in millions)

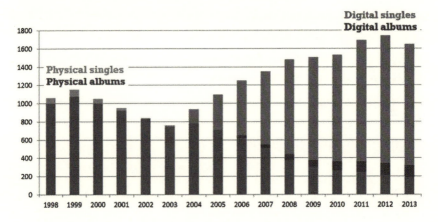

Here comes music streaming

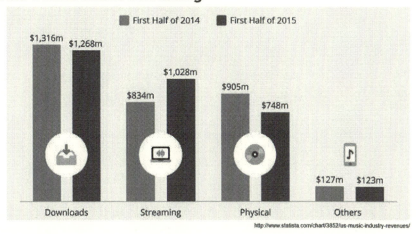

Artists derive very little income from the sales of their music in digital form. The exposure helps them reach a larger audience and establish a loyal fan base. They tend to make their money on tour. Taylor Swift topped the list of being the highest paid musician in 2018.[48]

Kent would love to get his music on Spotify playlists to reach potential new fans so that he can figure out the demographics of his fan base and then plan his shows in those locations. This would be a way he could turn his passion into income. For now at least, he doesn't count on selling his music for income but as a tool for marketing and discovering the most effective locations for his shows.

A Long and Winding Road

Kent has been working extremely hard on educating himself on song writing, music production, and networking. He has been investing in better equipment to achieve the sound he desires and that feels right for him. He is now coming to a point where he is loving the result of what he is working on. The road ahead is to get his projects completed and out to the right people and then take it from there.

---

48   Billboard's Money Makers: The Highest Paid Musicians of 2018.

MORE Breakthroughs

Kent is working towards his *lucky break*. He believes in first things first and that big breaks do not happen overnight. They are years in the making. Keep these thoughts in mind in the context of his following points.

M	Mindset	• If you don't have purpose in what you're doing, you will surely give up.
O	Opportunities	• Constantly seek out or create for yourself opportunities to grow your network, your knowledge and content to offer to the world. • When opportunities come, be ready. Don't let them take you by surprise and leave you saying, 'If I had more time, I would have been prepared . . .' (I'm no expert at this, but I'm always trying to better myself.)
R	Resources	• Invest in yourself, your equipment, your education, and your health. These are all responsible for your success and are needed to better your chance for a big break. • Make your next product while you are enjoying selling your last one. For musicians like me, while I play my music, I need to be writing more around the shows.
E	Energy	• Perform every show like they matter the same. • The very most you put into your content is the very most you'll get out ie if I write a song with 80% effort and wonder why it turned out badly, I can't be surprised and in fact, down the track, I realise I wasted my time. I'm better off putting everything into it, and if it still turns out badly, I know I'm not to blame and might just learn something and strengthen my writing ability.

At first, getting his hospitality and retail jobs certainly didn't feel like big breakthroughs, especially because he had worked so hard to finish his music degree and felt eager to get out and tour. Now looking back, Kent can see that these experiences taught him a lot.

He learned to communicate better and be disciplined with time so he can write or record or play gigs around his roster. With his earnings, he has invested in music equipment including some recording gear for his makeshift home studio, and gear to play live. He also attended some summer schools after completing his degree and has since worked through an online course learning music production to better his skills and knowledge.

Other massive breakthroughs include working with me and having the opportunity to play and record in Singapore. For one of his songs, Kent was actually paid enough to buy the MIDI keyboard he dreamed of getting. He has since used this keyboard for many projects, and it is one of the most important and consistently used parts of his studio.

Playing cover gigs in bars, corporate settings, weddings, shopping centres, and the like has really helped him to get some exposure for himself. He now needs to work on pleasing his fans with original content as well as connecting with new ones along the way.

Co-Lyricist

Being a co-lyricist has been a challenging yet rewarding experience. Having lyrics that already have their direction set in stone limits where Kent can go creatively, compared to his usual process for songwriting.

But it also helps in a way because there's less to consider in the starting process, and more focus can be given to refining the lyrics to make sure they have the ultimate impact on the listener both subconsciously and consciously. A good song should not rely entirely on the music to create feeling. It is nice to have the responsibility for this.

Rising Star: Watch Out For Kent Tonscheck

Kent plans to make 2020 a big year for progress, potentially rebranding with a stage name and having his demos professionally recorded and released. He has invested in dental work to have a more marketable image and a confident smile, has attended a songwriting summer school with Pat Pattison (who taught John Mayer), and has been writing and upgrading his equipment to create his signature sound. You could say he has been doing everything to make the stars align. The year 2020 looks like a successful year for Kent Tonscheck.

Gigs, concerts, studio sessions, tours, a label, and a producer would be nice future options. Kent does not discount owning a school of music in the future, perhaps when he has completed a few world tours and gotten sick of travelling. For now, it would be more of a distraction. Doing a few things well and working towards his breakthrough are the priority.

There is always a thrill in identifying a star before others see it and spotting Kent is one example. Cheers to Kent!

Reflections

ACES Criteria	Reflections
Do they fulfil dreams and passions?	
Do they create or capture value as per life's mission?	
Can the values and benefits be shared for the greater good?	
Do others judge the achievements as great? (Wow, you aced this!)	
Will they create a better future – legacy?	

8.0

Dare to Pursue

#Up to It

Most sports people who have given their formative years to represent their state or country in their sport invariably have to sacrifice their secondary school studies. This is also the crucial time in their teenage years to build their educational foundation and prepare for their future studies. The dilemma to choose a sport over studies is common. Their parents are equally concerned. The question they often ask is, is there a meaningful career after competitive sports? Is it possible to combine passion, interests, studies, career, and life goals together? If they are unsuccessful in reaching the right level in competitive sport, do they still have a future?

Some youngsters may be happy to sacrifice their studies if they are struggling in the first place. Most will have to delay their studies by three to five years, depending on their ability to climb the competitive sport ladder. Some may try to accommodate both studies and sports simultaneously. This requires significant discipline and sacrifice. National sports bodies are acutely aware of such issues and have tried to introduce different programmes in past years to address some of them.

Ex-Malaysian national shuttler Daphne Ng Chiew Yen understands this dilemma very well. She went through these crossroads that require careful deliberation, discussion, and decision. Thankfully, she found a way to combine the many goals of sport, career, and life together and became distinctive Daphne, the one who dares to pursue.

The Whole Is More than the Sum of the Parts

Daphne transitioned from an ordinary kid in a middle-class Malaysian family who grew up in Penang to being a competitive player with 11 career wins to being a badminton coach cum counsellor and now a consultant in the making. At age 17, she was the youngest player selected to join the National Back-up Squad and became a full-time badminton player. For these achievements, she is adored by her parents and has garnered many other admirers.

Daphne co-owns a badminton academy with her friend Sabrina Chong, who was once her roommate in the national team. Together, they are working diligently on this venture and are actively promoting it. As part of branding the academy, Daphne contributes to the local community, representing Malaysia in some of the national sports programmes and is now the Milo brand ambassador.

What has taken others a lifetime to develop, Daphne has achieved in a short time and at a young age. Her future is bright, building from this great foundation and platform. There is optimism and confidence of extraordinary growth and superior performance in her life journey. This story captures her passion in sports and how she has turned her passion into a business and career.

The whole is more than the sum of the parts – career wins.

The whole is more than the sum of parts (Sports Icon – Milo ambassador, Aktif Negaraku campaign)

Discipline and Diligence – Ingrained for Success

Successful athletes would not say that their successes are because they are lucky. To achieve mastery, they need an innate talent coupled with years of toil, sweat, perseverance, pain, and vigorous multidimensional training. In all of these, the right attitude, discipline, and diligence are key character ingredients.

Daphne learnt how to multitask early in her life. While most students could only focus on their studies and stop everything else before major examinations, she learnt to juggle both training and schooling, including preparing for her important national examination called Sijil Pelajaran Malaysia (SPM). Students in secondary schools are required to sit for this examination when they are 17 years old before proceeding to pre-university education if their results allow.

But Daphne went to a sports school instead of a regular school to combine training and studies in one. Her father, recognising that she still needed to pass her educational examination, hired a private tutor so that she could be taught the school educational syllabus during weekends and after training. The effort and sacrifice of sleep and a social life paid off when she completed and passed her examinations. She is now pursuing her doctoral studies, and this speaks well of her academic achievements.

The dilemma to choose sport over studies

Discipline and diligence as an athlete

Daphne's Diary Reflections

Notes from Daphne's diary: Never for a single moment have I regretted any session of practice, gymnasium training, or competitions. Even when I was having very serious injuries and very stressful competitive performance expectations, I still always reminded myself to stay positive and have a very strong belief in myself.

The amazing experience in peak performance sports is that I am able to feel the sweet satisfaction each time I win a point, a tournament, or even after I have performed my best. The desire I have for success, the friendships I have made through sports, the amount of personal and athletic growth I've experienced along the way have been monumental.

Daphne Day: Dawn to Dusk and Again

Her day starts early at dawn when she studies. This is the only time in the day she can pack in one to two hours of study before exercise and breakfast. She has completed her degree in Sports Science and Master's in Sports Science, majoring in Sports Psychology. She intends to extend her master's degree programme and proceed with research in sports coaching to achieve her ambition of completing her doctoral studies.

After completing her morning workout and breakfast, the day continues with managing her badminton academy, Duo Sparks. Coaching classes and clinics fill up most of the afternoons and evenings. A typical 'Daphne day' is 17 hours and ends at about 10.30pm, by which time, she is very tired. Weekends are just as busy. Coaching sessions begins as early as 7.30am right up to 6pm.

This demonstration of passion and commitment releases endless energy. She does not think she is working too hard even with her 17-hour daily schedule. Her passion is carrying her through, and each day is fulfilling. It speaks well of what people say about passion and energy. They are doing something they love, and they focus solely on doing what they love. Money and financial rewards are just by-products of what they love doing, and they work hard to achieve an excellent standard.

Is it sustainable? Well, so far so good.

Learning from Her Youngest Student and a CEO Student

We can learn from across the life spectrum, from the youngest to the most senior in the business and corporate world. We pick two students from Duo Sparks Academy to hear their feedback.

Youngest student: Alistair Chew, six years old

Is learning fun?	Yes.
Do you feel encouraged to learn how to play?	Yes, because when I win, I get medals.
Do you look forward to learning badminton compared to other classes?	Yes, because badminton is fun, and I get to sweat and be strong.

Successful businessman / corporate leader: Song Lg

How can you relate badminton and your work?	Through training in badminton, I overcome a lot of obstacles and disbelief about my ability and achieve certain results despite my age. I have applied this spirit, perseverance, and not giving up in my work. I have also gotten many breakthroughs as well.
How has coaching helped in achieving your objectives?	I have developed the spirit of persistence and endurance from the training sessions. My coach is patient and her belief in me has greatly boosted my self-confidence and self-esteem.
Any feedback on the style of coaching from your perspective?	I'm very happy with the method of coaching so far.

For the young, their requirement is simple. Make learning fun. For the experienced and successful executive, sport is a form of exercise and a chance to unwind and sweat away the stress. The training helps the brain to be agile and respond to the heavy demands of business and life.

Daphne 1.0, 1.5, and 2.0: Is There a Strategy?

Put simply, organisational strategy is a set of carefully selected (simply choice) plans and initiatives to be executed so that company objectives, aspirations, and goals can be achieved. Personal strategy extends the same business concept at the personal level. Reid Hoffman and Ben Casnocha encourage people to become the CEO of their own lives in their book, *The Startup of You*. In reality, people do set goals and pursue them at varying levels of intensity. However, most do not follow a systematic approach with strategy, unlike organisations that have to align and mobilise many stakeholders to achieve their objectives.

Has this *go-getter* Daphne had a personal strategy since young? She points to four different life stages, starting from the early years when she was 12–16 years old. In those years, there were no strategies other than following the directions and instructions of her parents and coach. It was more of going with the flow. They were instructions rather than guidance, which was right for that age. She did well in the Junior Badminton Circuit.

She describes her teenage years from 17 years to 20 years old as Daphne 1.0 or D1.0 in short, followed by young adulthood (D1.5 from 21 years to 26 years old), and now the current stage in her life, which she calls D2.0. Table 9.1 below outlines her own notes on her reflections on strengths-weakness-opportunities-threats (SWOT) in each of her life stages, her ACES and strategy. These so-called strategies ranged from ad-hoc and go-with-the-flow to deliberate thought-through strategies.

The hallmark achievement in her teenage years was Badminton Association Malaysia's (BAM) invitation to join the national badminton team. Her performance in her junior competitive circuit helped her to secure this prestigious achievement. Routines and lifestyle in the national team were predictable. It was training, studies, gymnasium exercises, and competitions. Goals were simple: Win as many competitions as possible and climb the ranking ladder. While pursuing this goal, she would fit in her studies as well. The ace is passing the important national examination as an independent student. This was probably a relief to everyone in the family.

Daphne 2.0 – thankful for my very supportive family and friends
They are the ones who inspire me in every way

Crossroads and Where to from Here?

A major life crossroads in her young adulthood stage was deciding whether to continue competitive badminton for a few more years or retire from the national team, pursue further studies, and explore her future career options. Reflecting on her SWOT analysis, she felt that she had to address some of the gaps in terms of business ventures when she started her badminton academy while pursuing her studies. This was seven years ago in 2012. Since then, every ounce of her energy is put into pursuing both studies and business.

Consistent with this book's theme of life *acts* on the world stage, Daphne's play script follows two lines of thinking. She was prepared to have a different lifestyle compared to other kids when she chose to join the national team at the onset. Second, she leveraged her prior platform and pursued new options as she transitioned into her next-life stage beyond competitive badminton. However, starting a badminton academy to coach and teach retired players is quite common. To differentiate herself, she pursued the corporate company segment in addition to consumer coaching. With the corporate segment, she introduces badminton as a game for sports, social leisure, team bonding, and changed management. This is gaining traction as society embraces employee wellness as a priority. Getting into the corporate network early has helped her advance towards her future goals.

Crossroads and where to from here Setting a new record in Malaysia Book of Records Promoting Badminton as a tool to embrace wellness

The Next Stage

Her next stage is D2.0. With the benefits of business school, experiences gained from running Duo Sparks, and a clearer sense of purpose over time, her strategies are becoming more succinct and clearer. Her goals include:

- completing her doctorate so that she can diversify her business portfolio and this includes the consultancy business
- expanding the business
- building her future personally and professionally

In general, millennials more than any other generation adopt technology in their lifestyle. She uses her social media channels extensively in her business. Her Facebook postings are helpful in understanding how and where she uses her time. The pursuit of knowledge and achieving her studies are well within grabs. Her business has steadily grown over the seven years, and her profile is improving. All these outcomes will help her achieve what she aspires in life.

Envision > Explore > Experience > Experiment > Evaluate

Oprah Winfrey, the famous American media executive cum actress and talk show host once said, 'Passion is energy. Feel the power that comes from focus and what excites you.' Daphne's family and friends will unequivocally agree that badminton is Daphne, and Daphne is badminton. These two nouns are interchangeable. Her top-of-mind recall on the answers to the interview questions below clearly demonstrate her passion for badminton.

Table 8.1 Transcript of the interview with Daphne Ng

	Interviewer	Daphne
1	Can you recall when you first picked up a badminton racquet?	Yes, I can. When I was six years old, my dad taught me badminton in the alley behind our home.
2	How and when did your interest start in badminton and subsequently become your passion?	I have just loved it since young. I would play on my own at home and hit the shuttle against the wall, even when there was no one to play with. I did not really know how to play at that time. When I was seven, my dad brought both my sister and me to a training academy for lessons. That was where we learned, and the journey continued from school to state and then landed me at the national level.
3	Can you remember your very first competition?	It was the MSSPP inter-school competition at 12 years of age.
4	Can you recall in which competition you achieved your first medal?	Wow! That was some time ago. Runner-up at the Penang Under-14 competition.

A good framework to help understand Daphne's process of thinking through her life-stage decisions is the 5E closed-loop framework of explore, experience, experiment, evaluate, and envision. The framework proposes:

Framework	Notes
Envision	Set aspirations, purpose, and goals.
Explore	Understand and explore the options systematically and as objectively as possible. Use SWOT to help think through the options.
Experience	Reflect on past experiences. Design with user experience in mind on future options.

Experiment	No pain, no gain. Have courage to experiment with some options.
Evaluate	Evaluate the outcomes. Check through the pros and cons.

Envision

Daphne aims to make sport and exercise fun, safe, and rewarding experiences for all.

In the next five years, Daphne's focus is to build her consultancy business in addition to her coaching academy. The business expansion programme will go beyond the region. She is actively building her business network and relationships as part of this expansion vision.

Both knowledge and skill are key for a consultant, and therefore, completing her tertiary studies, including the doctorate, add to her credentials and capability in badminton sports. Her specialisation is in the area of sports, health, and wellness development.

Explore

In the early years, Daphne was mostly a follower of instructions from her coaches and parents. The time to explore started when she decided to take on badminton as a career option. Duo Sparks is now seven years old.

Over the past few years, she has been exploring different channels and routes to build Duo Sparks's market eminence. She has volunteered and contributed to many social responsibility sports programmes, which often requires donating her personal time and effort.

Being a rookie in the world of business, she sought to learn from different sports experts and thought of options to differentiate Duo Sparks from an ordinary badminton-coaching school. This industry has low-entry barriers and is very competitive. She was very open minded and willing to try new ideas and concepts.

When exploring options, basic surveys and analyses on the size and competitiveness of the market were done before time and resources were invested to formulate the strategic responses.

Experience

As expected, there are good and bad experiences along the way. When Daphne was in the national team, it was training that mattered. Everything else was provided. Once in business, she was shocked by the negative views of athletes. Students joining the academy have expectations of being able to improve and compete, and the integrity of the competitive system comes into question. Fair play may be on the charter of many organisations that organise competitions, but these competitions may not necessarily be fair in execution. Persistence and tenacity to combat these systemic issues build character. When the students succeed and acknowledge the effort of the academy, it makes the success more valuable and provides the motivation for Daphne to carry on.

Experiment

One would hope that there is a guidebook to success, to be able to follow some steps and achieve a certain level of growth. Daphne has read her share of such books. In the end, it is a combination of many activities and initiatives, some more productive than others.

Identity and branding are important drivers when it comes to consulting. The hard work of representing the brand in social media, being present at many of the competitions, and saying *yes* to a lot of networking activities helped to build brand awareness and recognition when Duo Sparks was unknown.

Evaluate

Feedback loops are important to provide insights for improvement. Daphne makes it a point to get constant feedback on how she can improve in her business and study. She is fortunate enough to be chosen by various organisations to represent Malaysia on exchange forums to learn from the best.

5E – evaluate – chosen to represent Olympic Council of Malaysia for Chinese Olympic Committee Youth Camp in Beijing

5E– experience D 2.0 – Duo Sparks, an extraordinary badminton academy

'To err is human'

The fuller form of this proverbial phrase is 'To err is human; to forgive divine.' Alexander Pope, its originator, was trying to convey the point that all people commit sin and make mistakes. God forgives and people are acting in a godlike (divine) way when they forgive.

Daphne has had her share of disappointments and frustrations. The frustration as an athlete was when she lost in tournaments after putting on great performances. She trained very diligently every day over the years, and during competitions, it was really difficult to accept defeat.

Injury is a nightmare for an athlete. Daphne had a stress fracture in her fifth metatarsal in 2009 and had to repair her Achilles tendon in 2012. The recovery took almost one year, which forced her out of competition and training. It was an emotionally depressing time.

She also encountered bias in selection even after she had won all her matches. In several selections, she was not selected due to bias and favouritism. This could be very discouraging and disappointing for her.

The next stage – working towards more collaborations to encourage sports, health, and wellness

The Future Daphne

As a former athlete, Daphne believes in giving her upmost best and dedicating her life to the pursuit of excellence. These traits are important whether in sports, business, or life. Moving forward, she will leverage her strength in order to build an established brand. This is her focus in life right now. She is totally enjoying the journey, each and every day.

Dare to Pursue

Daphne loves travelling and seeing the world whenever she can. To her, this is the best way to learn, reflect, grow, and get inspired. During her days off, she enjoys reading, watching movies, and practising yoga. She cherishes moments spent with friends and family because she knows that without them she would not be who she is today. They build her in every way. Hers has been an incredible story of pursuit. Perhaps she should work now on reducing the length of her working day and spending more time on her social life.

It is hoped that the reader has gained some insights into a young lady who is successfully navigating her life and is always up for the next challenge.

Reflections

ACES Criteria	Reflections
Do they fulfil dreams and passions?	
Do they create or capture value as per life's mission?	
Can the values and benefits be shared for the greater good?	
Do others judge the achievements as great? (Wow, you aced this!)	
Will they create a better future – legacy?	

Average to ACES

Table 8.2 Daphne's Record of Her Badminton Journey

	ACES	Opportunity	Threat	Strategy	Strength	Weakness
Early years (12 to 16)	Student and Competitive Badminton	1. Supportive parents 2. Knowledge of the sports 3. Guidance from coaches		Initutive 1. go with the flow 2. passion drives 3. Intructed more than guided 4. Intercepted	1. Love sports 2. Active 3. Good personality	1. Lack of sports performance knowledge 2. Friends influence 3. Immaturity
Teenage (High School Age) (17 to 20)	Competitive Junior National Team	Chosen Badminton Association Malaysia (BAM) 2. Sports Scholarship 3. Attractiveness of Fame in representing Country	Unclear career path Threat of Injuries	1. Join National Body for competitive ladder opp 2. Pursue Vision 3. Excel in the sports	Clarity and Vision Parents' specific support Performance Peak	Distracted Low market profile (difficult to attract sponsors)
Young Adult hood (21-26)	Professional Player / Student Athlete	1. Grab every opportunity 2. Supportive friends and peers	1. Stressful 2. Difficulty dealing with clients and customers 3. Denial	1. Build essential business foundations 2. Build profile and expand influence 3. Build a trusted and respected identity	Knowledge and experience in badminton Good communication skills Willing to learn Persistence	Lack of business, coaching experience Limited resources
D2.0 (>26 to 35)	Coach / Consultant	To expand overseas beyond KL and Selangor	1. Leverage Network 2. Reach pinnacle of studies (doctorate)	1. Competition	1. Build essential business foundations 2. Learn the skills of entrepreneurship 3. Scale capacity thtough partnership 4. Find Investors	1. Good Market Profile 2. Determination to pursue this as career 3. Clear ambition	1. Time and Opportunities 2. Family and personal obligations

9.0

Copy Warrior Secrets

#Never take no for an answer and just do you

Ange Dove aka Copy Warrior is a professional copywriter and founder of the first and longest-standing copywriting agency in Singapore. She built her copy-warrior reputation by standing up for correct English and protecting her clients' corporate reputation, sometimes from themselves.

The Accidental Entrepreneur

Today, she is a seasoned business owner about to extend her business into the online education space, offering training courses to teach business owners to brand and market themselves through her signature programme Get Ready, Get Seen, Get Business. She is taking advantage of the opportunities that digital and Cloud technologies offer in this space. She has come a long way in her entrepreneurial journey and has come full circle in a way. But it all started as a bit of an accident, really, just because she wanted to work from home and look after her kids.

Ange's signature course

If you'd have told Ange 30 years ago, when she was a bank clerk in the UK, that she would one day own her own business or two, she would have laughed at the thought. It simply wasn't on her radar in the slightest. She had no model for it at all – not a business bone in her body.

No Business Model to Latch On To

Ange grew up an *armed-forces brat* and spent her formative primary school years living on the idyllic island of Malta in the Mediterranean Sea. Her father was posted there in the air force and her mother, previously a nurse, was a stay-at-home mum. This was Ange's model growing up, and all she ever wished for as a little girl was to be just like her mum. She saw her future as finding a husband and having children. She had no clear ambition to work as anything. Well, there was a brief desire to be a flight attendant since she loved the uniform of one particular airline. Later in her teen years in London, there was the dream to draw for a living. Her father encouraged this, seeing her talent for it, and suggesting she attend art college, but Ange rejected the idea for fear of not having a stable income. Growing up, all she knew was stability and the fear of not having money was real.

Moving back to the UK in 1978, after Malta had gained independence from the Commonwealth, Ange's world view didn't shift much. On leaving secondary school, she joined a bank and saw her time there as a temporary stop gap until that husband turned up and provided all for her. Nowhere in her community did she have access to business owners or entrepreneurs. Everyone was employed (or not) and worked from pay cheque to pay cheque, month after month. That was just the way things were in Ange's eyes. That was until she decided to take the opportunity to take on an English teaching job in Singapore back in 1993, just to work for 18 months as a chance to see the Far East. It was a departure for her, but she saw it as a short-term thing. In 18 months, she thought she'd be back in the UK and probably back working in the bank, still waiting on that husband.

A Brave New Entrepreneurial World

Coming to Singapore opened Ange's eyes to a whole different way of working. Many of the people she got to know ran their own businesses. Women had high-paying jobs in high positions in corporate companies. Everything worked. Everything was efficient and opportunities just seemed more possible.

Ange settled into teaching and discovered it to be extremely rewarding. She taught a mixture of different classes from businessmen in the evenings to kids, teenagers, and housewives in the daytime. Looking back on it now, she realises that part of the attraction was working autonomously, like running her own business in a way. It was her training wheels, if you like. She was employed by the school and had to follow a syllabus but was able to plan her own individual lessons however she wanted within that framework. And in the classroom, she was her own boss. She renewed her teaching contract at the 18-month mark and settled down in Singapore, eventually marrying and having two children.

Working from Home

Then the Internet came along and home computers enabled working from home. Ange immediately saw the opportunity to combine her language teaching knowledge with writing for a living and decided that providing writing services to businesses was a great way to earn money while working from home and looking after her two toddlers. At that time, she saw so many errors in printed materials and on retail signs, if only they would get that proofread! Then she read that to earn money, she needed to have a business. OK, my friends have their businesses, so why can't I?' she thought.

Working from Home Backfired

It was now 2003, and she headed straight down to ACRA to register her sole proprietorship (which she incorporated two years later) and set up her home office. Unfortunately, or rather fortunately, as it turned out, Ange's plans to work from home didn't quite work out. She ended up being in high demand and needed the support of additional admin and editorial staff to help her run what was becoming a flourishing business.

'I was a little freaked out when I took my first office,' Ange recalls. 'I had to commit to $1,000 a month rent and pay my three staff. I'd accidently built myself a business and painted myself into a job!'

Learning *on the Job*

The one thing Ange hadn't considered was that she had absolutely no experience in running a business, but she wasn't going to let that stop her. She hired a business coach at various points in the business growth to guide her and give her direction and encouragement. She also made her fair share of mistakes.

'I had no clue about keeping accounts so outsourced that to accountants and HR was a complete mystery to me. I made horrendous rookie mistakes in hiring staff, thinking I could train them if they didn't have the skills,' she recalls. 'My job interviews were a joke, but I soon realised that it caused far less stress to hire staff who were already experienced. I got really good at writing targeted job ads that filtered applicants that wouldn't suit.'

Ange learned well from her mistakes and looked back on them as golden learning opportunities. 'When you make mistakes, you are much more likely to learn from the pain and the hardships than to remember and take in theory from a textbook. Experience is a much better teacher.'

Can You Do Twice as Much for Half the Price?

Another challenge for Ange in the early days was negotiating fees with clients. She came from the UK, where prices were fixed and not negotiated. You either accepted the price offered or you walked away. Bargaining was considered cheap and demeaning. It was like admitting you couldn't afford something. 'So, you can imagine my surprise and disdain when I was first confronted with a customer bargaining!' Ange laughs.

In the early days, she gave in far too easily and ended doing jobs for way less than the fee she deserved. But she soon established a figure for each service below which she wouldn't go as it didn't make business sense. Once she had this figure established, she became confident in bargaining and walking away when the asking price was too low. 'I remember one particular project where I quoted a fair price and the client wanted me to slash it in half. Since I was already sure my stated price was fair to both parties, I flatly refused to bargain and kept to the original price quoted. Within one minute of that refusal email, the client scanned across his signed acceptance of the original quote. Talk about trying your luck!'

The Importance of Branding

Over time, Ange was able to build a solid brand both for her company Proof Perfect and for herself, which made bargaining almost a thing of the past. In fact, the opposite started to happen with clients calling and saying, 'I don't think I can afford you, but can you quote for …?' This experience made Ange aware of the importance and power of branding – of creating a desired perception so that you can command a higher price. Of course, with that comes the need to deliver value.

The Dark Days of the Recession

But one thing Ange didn't bank on was a recession and having a brand could only protect you so far. The 2008 recession hit the business hard. 'It was as if someone had flicked a switch,' Ange recalls. 'We went from business as usually to getting no enquiries at all, overnight! I remember sitting over lunch with one of my entrepreneur friends and telling her, 'I've got fixed overheads of $15,000 a month and sales so far this month are $1,000. What am I supposed to do?"' Ange had never been in this situation before.

'It was really stressful. I started by negotiating the rent with the landlord, who was really lovely and supportive, and putting my existing staff on part-time contracts, hoping that things would blow over and we'd get back to normal. Unfortunately, and quite understandably, those staff didn't feel so secure and looked for more secure employment elsewhere, so within a few months I was completely on my own,' says Ange. 'My mortgage was in arrears, credit card debts mounted to the max, and I even lost two savings policies because I couldn't make the last monthly instalment to allow them to keep running by themselves. It was a mess. But I struggled on. I just took the view that I had to make it work.'

Ange attributes this thinking to the same entrepreneur friend she had lunch with. This friend ran a graphic design agency and had hit some tough spots growing her business too, growing too large too fast at one point and having to let go of staff. Then at one point, rents spiked drastically, taking her office rent from $3,000 a month to $9,000 overnight. Ange asked her why she didn't move out and find somewhere cheaper and her friend's answer has stuck with her to this day, 'We've invested too much in the interior design to move out. We'll just have to make more money per month.'

It was that simple – make more money. So any time Ange hit cash flow issues, she remembered her friend's comment and got to work making more money!

Floating on the Cloud

Ange also kept an eye on developing technology and got really excited to see how it could streamline her business. The Cloud was an amazing invention to her, and she couldn't understand why other small businesses were so slow to adopt it. Her experience with such technology started with her desire to have a CRM back in 1995 before the Cloud and apps became a thing. She started with an offline version at first but when apps became available, Ange investigated what worked easily with the business and soon employed, on an SAAS subscription-based model, a CRM app, a HR app, a time management app, an accounting app, a marketing app, and a project management app – all running on the Cloud. She found ways to integrate them all so that work didn't have to be duplicated during data entry, and the project workflow was automated.

Making Global Connections Working Location Free

Working location free - must have coffee!

Moving the business to the Cloud enabled Ange to work from anywhere in the world with an Internet connection and at any time. It was an exciting time to be in business. She found that she could visit family in the UK and still run the business a couple of hours a day. She could attend conferences around the world, and she also found it exciting to connect to like-minded business owners in other countries. She became good friends with an Irish lady running the same kind of business as her after being paired with her as an accountability buddy on an online course. She made friends with a lady in Florida after commenting on her marketing during an online challenge they were both taking part in. Messenger conversations led to a friendship and a possible meetup in Florida in 2020! These are just a couple of many friendships developed online.

Growing by Answering Client Demands

Ange held strong values around customer service, stemming back from her days in the bank, where customer service was the only differentiating factor between one bank and another. She was determined to add value for her clients and always went above and beyond to deliver the unexpected. She listened to what clients wanted and soon found that she was adding on design services to her copywriting solutions. As the demand grew, she brought in design staff in-house, and by 2016, her agency, operating from a shophouse in Kampong Bahru Road, had ten staff offering the full range of marketing solutions.

Is It Really Worth It?

Overheads were high, mostly salary expenses and rent, and more money had to be made just to cover those expenses. 'It got to the point where expenses were just too high, and I wasn't bringing in enough to cover them. I have to be honest: This was the worst time in my business – worse than the 2008 recession. I wasn't enjoying coming to work at all. The responsibility of trying to secure jobs for the staff was debilitating and for the first time in the running of Proof Perfect, I really considered jacking it all in. I was exhausted.' It was at times like this that Ange relied heavily on her online community of business buddies.

Transitioning to a Virtual Business Model

Around the same time, Ange had started looking into online courses and built her business and marketing skills by attending quite a few of them. One of the gurus she came across was a woman who had built a successful business on Facebook for free, run completely online. Ange loved this business model and quickly recognised that it was the answer she had been looking for to keep Proof Perfect running and to add on to her services through running her own online training courses.

She put together a plan and worked it in stages. Firstly, she halved her rent and utility costs by moving from the shophouse to a serviced office with five hot desks. With the business already operating on the Cloud, Ange knew that she didn't really need a physical office at all. So she set the office up so that staff could work in the office on a first-come-first-served basis at the hot desks or in the common areas of the serviced office space or work from home. Some staff embraced the change and welcomed being able to work from home, and others rejected it completely and moved on. Instead of replacing staff that left, Ange sourced for talent online that could offer the same service on a per project basis.

Within two years, she was able to give up the physical office space entirely and had transitioned to a purely online team located around the globe. Now she had very low fixed overheads – just for a retained admin staff, app subscriptions, and one full-time writing staff and full-time design staff. All the rest were outsourced as needed on a secure platform on the Cloud designed for handling the outsourcing of projects.

'It was so liberating to be able to harness technology in this way and completely change my business model. I'm still waiting for mainstream businesses to catch up. Answering the question, "How big is your company?" is still a problem as most just don't get it. Size is more than the physical number of staff you employ. The way business is done has changed. You just have to look at the major companies operating today – Airbnb rents out spaces yet owns no property. Grab, Uber, and Lyft offer taxi rides but own no vehicles. Shared office space is becoming the norm. It's a sharing economy.'

Paying It Forward

Having stabilised Proof Perfect to be run by her staff on the Cloud, Ange is now turning her energies to the next chapter in her life, her training arm MarketSMART Learning Hub. 'What I am incredibly passionate about is using technology to help small business owners like me to market and strengthen their business themselves – empowering them with the knowledge, through my online training courses and coaching programmes, to be able to do it all themselves. I just got so sick of hearing business owners say they were at the mercy of marketing agencies, didn't know what was going on, and weren't seeing the desired results. I had been in the same place and I worked out how to use technology to build and market my own brands and I built a viable online training business doing what I love and helping fellow business owners do the same. I help those who are now where I used to be to get to where I am now. I just teach what I know and help people build their business and personal brand and position, promote, and profit from doing what they love. Life's too short to be spending your days doing something that doesn't interest you and doesn't fulfil you. The Internet and Cloud technologies have completely enabled this liberating way of doing business, and I want to empower more business owners to do the same.'

MarketSMART Learning Hub

Ange's courses were built drawing inspiration from her long entrepreneurial journey. She struggled in her early days of business with having no personal brand. She wasn't even featured on her own business website for many years. 'I think about all the money I must have left on the table by not pushing my brand in the early day,' she says. 'I don't want other business owners to make the same mistake. It took me a long time to build the confidence to establish my brand.' She went from not having any photos taken of herself to getting very comfortable getting in front of the camera on video and even on webinars, something she never thought she'd master. 'Now I love webinars!' she says. 'This is really my platform of choice today.'

Just Do You

What stopped Ange from building her brand initially was thinking she had to copy those who were already successful. 'I didn't realise I should just be my authentic self. But the reality is, there is only one me. There is only one you. If you are true to yourself, and accept yourself, you will find an audience that resonates with you, and that's your tribe.'

Ange's training in action.

Today, Ange helps small business owners and coaches find their online tribe and build a business by meeting the specific needs of their tribe. She is a perfect example of sheer grit and determination trumping knowledge and experience and of faking it until she makes it. She is proof that taking the copy-warrior approach to doing business leads ultimately to triumph.

Reflections

ACES Criteria	Reflections
Do they fulfil dreams and passions?	
Do they create or capture value as per life's mission?	
Can the values and benefits be shared for the greater good?	
Do others judge the achievements as great? (Wow, you aced this!)	
Will they create a better future – legacy?	

10.0

Purpose, Peace, and Progress

#DiamondCut

It was my usual travel routine. I had checked in my luggage and was heading towards customs when I heard my name being called from behind me. I turned around and noted a familiar frame pacing towards me. It was Gao Li, a member of staff that I had mentored during my long professional career with Deloitte. We exchanged formalities and decided to catch up over coffee since we both had ample time before our flights.

Merely a Speckle Out of a Billion (十亿分之一)

Gao is a first-generation Chinese migrant to Singapore. He was born into a working-class family in China, where the population then was slightly over a billion. The country was still very much socialist in nature. The year that Gao was born was the first time China was introduced to Western consumerism when KFC first opened its first store in China.

Post Chairman Mao, a new pragmatic leadership under Deng Xiaoping emphasised economic reform and targeted expanding rural incomes. Moving from the days of a planned economy, with rationed household goods and foods, China was progressing towards an enterprise autonomy, reducing central planning and attracting foreign direct investments into China. Gao was born amidst the drastic cultural shift, when the Chinese were starting to become inquisitive about what was behind the closed doors of Chinese society.

Also in the 1980s, China introduced what is arguably the most extreme population planning programme in the world, the 'One Child Policy'. Under this policy, provincial governments created propaganda campaigns to encourage families to limit births to one child and slapped enormous fines on families that were non-compliant to this policy. It was reported that more than 400 million babies were prevented through this programme, which created a generation of little emperors.

The common perception is that the little emperors are spoiled, narcissistic, and unable to do anything without adult intervention and that they have attention lavished on them not just from their parents, but also their grandparents. However, what most people fail to consider is the amount of pressure these children had to shoulder at a very young age. In a culture where children have to fund their parents' retirement, the pressure to succeed can be quite daunting. Gao recounts, during his earlier years of schooling, that everyone in the family was investing all their energy and resources to make sure he could excel. Academic grades were the only priority, as it was seen as the only route to break away from mediocrity. The single child was often the single chance they had.

Gao first moved to Singapore in the 1990s.

On Paving Ways for the Future (前人栽树, 后者乘凉)

Gao used to run my business development function back in Deloitte. I noticed he exhibited more entrepreneurial spirit compared to some of his peers. He was a self-starter, always taking initiatives and finding new ways of solving problems. To this, he credited his parents.

Gao's parents were assembly line workers in a state-owned transformer manufacturing company. They were born in the 1960s and went through the Cultural Revolution. They were taught that being intellectual was akin to being a capitalist – the *evils* within the socialist society. His parents were uneducated and spent much of their school years in mass rallies and carrying out manual work. The ideology imparted to them was that physical laborious hard work was the only way out of poverty.

So as ordinary factory workers, they put in a lot of hard work. They would work a 60-hour work week, and signed up at every opportunity to work overtime. Gradually, they accumulated a small amount of wealth between them and would spend a portion of it on their inquisitiveness of Western culture. They would queue for hours for movie tickets to watch the latest Western films at the only theatre in their city, which in the 1980s was considered a luxury.

Through the influences of Western culture, the young couple associated foreign lands with a better life, and soon incepted ideas to leave China for good. This was by no means a small feat, especially for a working-class family. They looked for various ways to achieve their goals, looking for loopholes and opportunities to get out of the country. The day finally came in 1994. Gao's mom took him on a one-way trip to Singapore, where his new life was about to begin.

Fitting in, for Survival

Life in this new country started out a little rough for Gao, who was only seven years old, when he migrated. Singapore was foreign to him in almost every way. He knew not a single word of English and struggled at even memorising the 26 letters of the alphabet. He was like a fish out of water.

He shared with me that the first day he attended school, he had to sit for a test. It was a simple one, which was to label the human body parts, yet he did not know a thing and was lost as to where he should start. Back in China, Gao was always a top student. He would often achieve 95 marks and above in his tests and examinations. Anything less was unacceptable by his family's standards. Being fearful that his family would be disappointed, he resorted to cheating. Yet he still only managed 65 marks.

Very soon, he realised scoring A was the least of his concerns. He had a bigger issue to deal with. Being the new kid in school, he became an easy target for bullying. He recalled, 'I was called names that I didn't understand until I searched the dictionary at night.' He recounts that those days were tough, and it continued in the same way pretty much for the early years of his time in Singapore.

Refusing to see this as a setback and submitting to his predicament, he started making additional effort to learn the language. His trick to remember the pronunciation of words his teachers taught was by jotting down the Hanyu Pinyin for ease of memory. It worked well for him.

Beyond that, he started looking for friends who were more well-versed in Mandarin. He said he got his first ever group of friends in Singapore *(they are still friends by the way)* through *bribing* them using two bottles of Pepsi and snacks. He was concerned that his friends would still find him weird, so he started mimicking how his friends behaved and tried to adopt the same hobbies and interests so that he could keep his friends. Gradually, he became more confident and started to find opportunities at social gatherings to make more friends. At gatherings, he found ways to make his friends accept him, be it by making jokes of himself, giving the group a good laugh, or accepting general consensus of the group, even though he didn't always agree.

Fitting in at all cost was his modus operandi growing up. This was his survival instinct. It was a way he could have a life in a foreign land.

Gao seen here with his basketball teammates. Some of them went on to represent Singapore in International Competitions (2003)

Gao volunteered for an overseas community involvement programme to help build houses in rural Kunming (sometime between 2005 and 2006).

Gao acted in a play adapted from the musical *Fame* as Joe Vegas (2008).

Gao seen here with his rugby team and their trophy (2009)

The Sharp Edge of the Sword (物极必反)

His survival instincts got him through his early teenage years. He never had issues making friends. But this was soon not enough for Gao, especially as he entered tertiary education.

University is the place where teenagers transit to become adolescents. It is often the first time that they taste freedom, with very little parental supervision, and lots of new opportunities open up. And tertiary education in Singapore was unique because the boys enter university fresh off their national service. This is the prime time for any Singaporean male. The boys were ripped and masculine, and there was plenty of competition for attention and popularity.

He knew he wanted to be that alpha male – that popular guy! Across his four years of university life, he took on all sorts of opportunities to stand out. In the freshmen year, he was nominated for a pageant contest, where he got two out of the three available prizes, including the winner of the pageant. He took on modelling gigs and did cameos in TV series. He played a bunch of competitive sports, including badminton, basketball, and rugby, where he captained the team to the championship. He also acted and directed in plays, took on gigs as an emcee, kick started a small T-shirt business to gather funds for his dorm, and took part in all sorts of other co-curriculum activities, all without compromising his studies. He successfully graduated from Nanyang Technological University, one of the top 20 universities in the world and landed a job in a big 4 accounting firm.

Gao felt like he was unstoppable. He felt that the world was his oyster and that he could eat it for breakfast, lunch, dinner, and supper. He was addicted to the feeling of being popular and achieving what his peers saw as accomplishment. He felt that this must be it, his way of life. Little did he realise that the adult world was way more complex than he had imagined. The set of criteria to define popularity and accomplishments was so different. Many of his friends went on to become bankers and had conversations around the banking industry, of which he knew nothing about. Some of those conversations usually ended up being banters comparing how much each of them was making every month.

Gao felt lost and soon found himself having to navigate through a new but more sophisticated set of social rules and conversational topics, sometimes taking on way more than he could chew.

He struggled to fit in again. However, he refused to give in. He looked for other ways to be accepted, which he found through social drinking. Going for happy hour and having a beer or two was part of his everyday life. After a couple of glasses of alcohol, pretty much everything would be no holds barred. There was plenty of laughter and fun, and all differences seemed to be cast away. The feeling was exhilarating, and he loved it. One or two glasses eventually led on to one or two bottles. The memories of fun eventually led to the loss of memory due to excessive drinking. The enjoyment of social companionship soon led to regret the next day as he nursed a massive hangover.

He was hooked. He found himself addicted to alcohol, something he could not control. He spent his entire salary on alcohol and parties, often finding it difficult to meet his financial needs at the end of the month. Gao could not control his alcohol intake. He told me that there was an instance where he woke up in hospital with four stitches on his right eyebrow and had no recollection of what had happened. This addiction took him on a downward spiral. He was leading a life without direction and without an identity. He was lost.

Gao and his family having lunch at NTU. His family was really proud that he went to one of the top universities in the world.

The Frivolous Search

Gao's lifestyle had a detrimental impact on his relationship with his mother, the single constant in his life. She had invested her whole life in taking care of him, especially after her divorce in the early 1990s. They often had heated arguments, which would end with his mom in tears. They were both heartbroken, and Gao knew he had to pick up the pieces somehow. He thought finding a girl to start a family with would lead him to being more grounded and less frivolous. It would give him a new purpose and direction. So he set out on a path to seek that someone.

He dated constantly and getting someone attracted to him was not an issue. Most of his dates would turn out to be good companions. They had common interests, and they shared wonderful memories together. When the relationship got serious, discussions would be had about longer-term commitment, Gao would always find excuses to brush it aside. He told me, 'Maybe I never wanted a family. Maybe I just wanted to get my shit sorted out.' His attempt to seek stability became a solution to his issues, but deep down he knew that this was not what he wanted. He still wanted to be free. As you may have guessed, after two or three failed attempts at building a stable relationship, he went back to his lifestyle of partying and hardcore alcohol.

Gao seen here with me when I nominated him for the Best Trainer Award in Deloitte

Finding Ground on Foreign Soil

Sometime in 2017, an opportunity presented itself for Gao to move to Thailand. It was a good career move and took some attention off wanting to fix his alcohol addiction. Moving to a foreign country did not scare him this time around as it did when he was eight years old. In fact, he was eager. Although he had travelled to various countries in the past for work, ranging from exotic countries like Nepal, Sri Lanka, and Turkey to developed countries like the United States, Hong Kong, and China, this time was different. This was a permanent move, and he would need to assimilate into a new culture.

The first few months in Thailand seemed all so familiar to Gao, as if he was brought back to when he first moved to Singapore. English literacy in Thailand was low, and most of the people spoke only Thai. He struggled to communicate. Even getting hold of daily necessities became a challenge. Because he had moved to Thailand alone, he had no friends and was starting anew.

The familiar circumstances made Gao reflect on his life and his alcoholism. He came to realise that, throughout his life, many of the things he did was to serve other's expectations. He was always seeking external validation to find out if he was right. When he was young, he studied hard and got good grades because that was what his family wanted. There was always this baggage on his shoulders to deliver results. Having the opportunity to be brought to Singapore by his family was a rare one, and it took years of hard work. He did not want to disappoint his family. Not quickly learning the language was never an option. The validation was of course the proud faces of his family when he managed to get into the schools that they wished him to go to.

Growing up, everything he did was to serve his social circles. Being good looking wins you attention, they say. Being great at sports wins you more friends, they say. He was often being strung along by what his friends and society expected of him. Rarely, he had the opportunity to pause and ask himself, 'What do I really want to be?' As a result, he was always making the convenient choice, to go along with his friends' decisions, and that made him popular. He received the validation needed from his social circles.

It all got worse when he started working. Conversations with friends were hidden with tinges of competition, each trying to show off by outperforming the other. In this regard, he told me he always felt that he was behind his peers. He wanted to be equally established and successful in his career, if not more, just so that he could feel that he belonged. Gao was feeling inferior and had placed huge pressure on himself to deliver the success he had defined for himself, which was money. He worked extra hours, found opportunities that would generate extra income, and tried to move up the corporate ladder as soon as he could. In so doing, he did not realise that this was the reason for his downward spiral.

He reflected, 'I learnt that alcohol was my escape. Before I drank, I had goals to reach, work to do. But after I drank, there seemed like no goal was too high to overcome, or so I thought. I was addicted to this feeling, and not the alcohol. Now reflecting back, it was silly because I had forgotten that, once I sobered up, the problems would still be there. I had not moved an inch closer to the goal I had set for myself.'

He was so consumed by these vanity expectations that his social circle was pressuring him to live up to that he almost lost his own identity. He was a man that his family had made him out to be, his friends had made him out to be, but hardly what he really wanted to be. This realisation hit him hard, and he knew it was time to change how things were working in his life.

The Transformation (蜕变)

Gao started by first being more truthful to himself and accepting that he had f–cked up. He stopped being in denial and finding excuses to run away from his own problems. He told himself, temporarily escaping his issues was only going to make that issue stay, not fix it. So he started working on his drinking habit. On regular days, he had a habit of drinking a pint of beer over dinner, and he wanted to cut down. He substituted it with soda water, which gave him similar fizzy sensations and enjoyment. Also, because he was in Thailand, away from his regular khakis, the opportunities to go on social drinking sessions were reduced, and as such, he was also able to binge drink a lot less often.

The next thing he started working on was his weight. By this time, because of all the excessive drinking, sleepless nights and ill-disciplined diet, he had gained more than 20kg since his university days. He was almost 100kg at his peak. Early warning signs of health problems linked to obesity surfaced. He started working on reducing his weight and improving his fitness. He started exercising daily. He downloaded an app to keep track of the daily exercises he was doing. It did not start off with daily one-hour runs, but simple targets of stretching for 15 minutes and 30 push-ups a day. Using the app as an external reminder, he felt like he had to commit to the habit and dutifully complete the tasks every day.

The last area he worked on was his mental wellness. He did two things: He took up meditation and mindfulness training every day before bed for ten minutes, basically setting aside some quiet moment for himself to reflect on the day that has passed. He re-enacted the happenings of the day, the happy and unhappy stuff, and let them run through their mind without having to keep them there. By doing so, he let go of the pressure of keeping those unhappy memories within him, especially as they could eventually escalate to stress. He worked pretty well, his temperament became better, and he had better sleep. The other thing he did was to start reading. Through the time spent nursing a hangover daily, he realised he had not really put in effort to make himself wiser and more knowledgeable. He started off with self-help books to guide him on the journey of transformation, then to business-related books to help strengthen his professional skills.

A Work in Progress

Gao told me, 'I see my life as a work in progress, and I want to keep moving forward.' At the time of writing this chapter, Gao is still working on his transformation. Through changes in lifestyle, he lost

12kg in less than a year. There was no extreme dieting, crazy-hard fitness plan, but only consistent, progressive, small changes every day. He picked up a new hobby, Muay Thai, which he finds to be a great stress reliever. He practises two times a week and spars with his coach to stay sharp and agile.

He has also moved onto a new job in a business dealing with transforming the healthcare industry, by using technology to give more access, affordability, and quality healthcare to everyone. It is definitely not a job that pays the most, but he finds a strong, compelling purpose to working on this for the good of mankind. As a result of his international experience, he now has a role in bridging communications between various countries and cultures. At the same time, he founded a start-up company to incubate ideas to help the construction industry transform itself through artificial intelligence. He boasts Kajima, one of the biggest Japanese construction companies, as one of his clients.

Gao still drinks on social occasions, which he tells himself is OK. But now he knows his limit, he can actively make decisions on how much he should drink and tries to avoid binge drinking. He is also focused on doing his part for the environment, making small efforts day by day to make sustainable life choices. He attempts to consume less, including having vegan days once a week.

Most important of all, through this whole process, he has finally found his life partner. He told me with some tears in his eyes, 'My wife inspired the positive change in me. She was a certified coach and was able to help me see perspectives beyond my own. I like it that I am better with her.'

They are due to get married in Bangkok in the spring of 2020.

Defining the *Ace*

Looking at Gao's story, he is just about as average as anyone can be. In fact, he represents most young adults growing up in Singapore. A lot of them are under similar pressures under the Asian parenthood regime, easily impressed by vanity metrics, and many get lost at one point or other in their lives.

His story reminds us to pause and reflect on ourselves, to find out where the true North Star is, and define your own success and fulfilling life.

The world is full of distractions these days. There are a million things fighting for our attention. We will get lost in trying to meet the expectations set on us. We might even get lost in technology. With the paradox of progress, new problems will always emerge. We should take some time for ourselves regularly to get reacquainted with our inner self, focus inwards, and ask the questions, 'How am I different from the other speckles of cosmic dust in the universe?'

'How would I define my *ace*?'

Gao posing for Uniqlo's Airism campaign

Gao seen here with his fiancée, working out together, trying to keep fit

Reflections

ACES Criteria	Reflections
Do they fulfil dreams and passions?	
Do they create or capture value as per life's mission?	
Can the values and benefits be shared for the greater good?	
Do others judge the achievements as great? (Wow, you aced this!)	
Will they create a better future – legacy?	

Living Better Lives

11.0

Average to ACES

#Mission JY: Create and Capture Value

The previous chapters are a collection of stories. The consistent theme across them is the journey from average beginnings to extraordinary achievements. It is about each person's pursuit of their dreams, passions, or success. Along the way, there are the mountain-high and valley-low episodes. Success or significance are relative. What are heartening are the common elements in these journeys for us to learn from. Now it is my turn. I will share my story over the following two chapters.

Average in My Beginnings

My beginnings are humble in many respects. Born into a low to middle-income family, my father was a salesman who lost his job in his early fifties and then passed away when I was 17. My family's financial circumstances were considered better compared to my older siblings' time. My father had different bouts of sicknesses, and there were times when the family survived from 'hand to mouth'. My mother, a homemaker, had always been resourceful and, on one occasion, had to sell some cooking oil to another tenant so that there was pocket money for my brother to go to school. I remember my father borrowed my entire savings of 70 ringgits on one occasion to pay some bills. He did return the money subsequently, much to my relief. I was 12 then.

Tasty *black noodles* was my favourite breakfast from the local market in my growing up days. It cost ten Malaysian cents. Today, it is still my favourite breakfast at about S$3 at the hawker centre.

My early school experience was not pleasant. While it is a norm for kids to attend pre-school today, I did not have any pre-school preparation. So when I started school, I had no idea what the teacher was teaching. To this day, I can still remember the red rectangle drawn in my book with the word *soap* on it. I muddled along and improved.

Diligence has always been my trademark. Although school results were average in my younger days, this character trait has since enabled me to complete several tertiary qualifications. Years ago, I sometimes would wake up in a cold sweat in the middle of the night worried that I was not ready for my pre-university examinations. This was years after I was working and had successfully completed my studies. Of course, I realised it was just a nuisance nightmare, another one of those psychological stress traumas from prior years. Thankfully, those nightmares have since left me and become a thing of the past.

After completing my first degree, I stayed behind in Australia for another year to pursue further studies. It was a legitimate way to stay on, find some work, and save for a car. Little did I know that the skills acquired from my postgraduate Diploma in Education was helpful in conducting training at various workplaces. When I applied for my first job, the finance manager gave me a supervisory role when he saw on my resume the various roles I had taken responsibility for in different student bodies. With the salary from my part-time work and savings from various summer vacation jobs, I was able to purchase my first pre-loved car. A new car in the 1980s amounted to 14 months of a fresh graduate's salary compared to 38 months of a fresh graduate's salary 35 years later.[49] Although affordability then was much better, I could only afford a pre-loved car.

I was keen to invest as soon as I started work. My small savings went towards my car purchase, and therefore, the deposit for a smaller house in a humble neighbourhood had to be borrowed from my mother. I had very little disposable income in the early years because I made it a point to repay my mother the deposit within three years with interest. After all that sacrifice, unfortunately, the investment was loss making. That was *tuition fee* into my world of property investment. Thankfully, the returns since then have been rewarding.

The World Has Changed and Continues to Change

The world has changed with the advancement of each industrial revolution, starting with the First Industrial Revolution in the 1760s. It was the era when machines replaced hand production to make way for mass manufacturing. Today, we are into the Fourth Industrial Revolution, where work can be performed anywhere and anytime because of the Internet invention. Obviously, with each industrial revolution comes the need to reskill and change in response to the new environment. People and society have successfully adopted and adapted with changes over time.

---

49 Hans, 'Then and Now, How Car Prices Have Changed – 1980 to 2015', 25 June 2015.

Figure 11.1 Industrial Revolutions

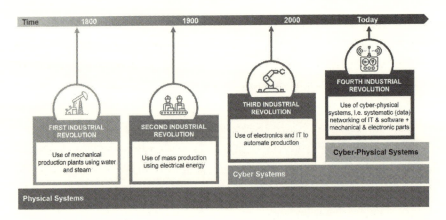

In the 1980s, it was the Third Industrial Revolution, where use of electronics and IT to automate production was the then new normal. Telex machines, typewriters, facsimile machines (fax), and mainframe and clunky personal computers were the main communication tools when I first joined the workforce in that period.

Fast-forward 30 years into the decade of 2010–2019, telex machines, and electronic typewriters are only found in museums to serve as a reminder of history. Job types such as typists are displaced and replaced by new job types such as data scientists and many new C-suite roles. Smart devices, powerful tablets, and the Internet dominate many aspects of our personal, social, and business life today. Like in previous industrial revolutions, job types continue to change. Disruptive technology such as artificial intelligence (AI) and machine learning (ML) will make devices smarter, and some jobs that are routine and manual will be displaced. The concern of machines totally replacing humans is unlikely. As in the past, some jobs will disappear, and new ones will emerge. The key is having the right skills to fit. This is why upgrading skills in a career continuum is important. Jobs requiring human judgement, experience, and cognitive skills are not easy to automate and are likely to increase in demand. Human and digital technology will coexist and work together.

ACES and My World Stage

My good friend penned these four Chinese words, 平步青云 (Píngbùqīngyún) in my autobiography. The phrase means small and ordinary steps (even steps). Those I have taken over the years have helped propelled me to ACES and prominence (clouds). In order to assess whether achievements are ACES, I developed a set of criteria to assess them. You will have seen that this set of criteria is included in the table at the end of each story chapter. You are encouraged to reflect on the journey and achievements of each person and pen what is applicable from their story to the five criteria so that the insight can be applied.

Past learnings and practice have helped me make better decisions and achieve more successful implementations. Despite the changes in an ever-evolving world, some learnings that helped build success are evergreen and they include:

- supporting and rooting for dreams to become real
- having life paradigms and value
- working hard
- playing hard
- being yet wiser

Dreams and aspirations played a big role in driving my behaviours. Life paradigms played a crucial part in how I approached work and investment and in how resources such as energy and time were invested. 'Work Hard, Play Hard' and 'Be Yet Wiser' are self-reflections of my journey. Besides formal learning, the school of hard knocks (informal learning through experience) was a good teacher. Bringing all the learnings together in one integrated package was key to answering the question, *Who am I?* I developed this framework to graphically present the five components of success.

Figure 11.2 Who Am I?

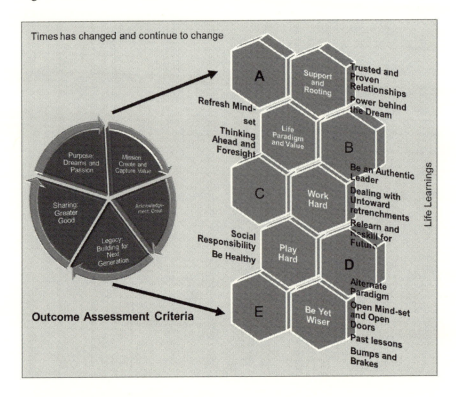

Support and Rooting for Dreams to Become Real

Humans are social beings and we constantly draw on love, support, and help from our family, friends, network, and society. As much as we like to be independent, we end up depending on each other from the cradle to the grave.

Leverage Resources from Trusted and Proven Relationships

Family support is often taken for granted. On reflection, my success in many endeavours was due to support and encouragement from family and help from trusted relationships. The neighbourhood where I grew up was less than glamorous. While my siblings' relationships ranged from cool to close, my brothers did step up when it mattered. The younger ones had the protection from the older siblings in this rough neighbourhood. Over the years, confidantes and mentors too have positively influenced my life and career, and these relationships have proven to be reliable.

My third brother was the first child in the family to study overseas. The award of a Colombo Plan scholarship made his dream of an overseas education possible. With that breakthrough, he started the brother-sponsor-brother scheme, which saw his younger siblings benefiting and building a future for themselves. This family micro-financing system proved effective. Not all families have the resources to support the economic needs of their next generation, and I was definitely a beneficiary.

Losing my father at 17 years old, just before my national high school examination, was stressful. My mum soldiered on to look after my younger brother and me, who were still at schooling age. Although not highly educated, her piousness and support were instrumental to my success. I wrote a song in honour of my mother, 'Everyone Has Heroes'.

Dreams Become Reality and the Power behind Them

Dreams and passions are motivating drivers. Steve Jobs (Apple) once said, 'Dream big.' Success is a result of many things done right and many right things implemented. Be a dream chaser. To do so, one must first have a dream and pursue it passionately.

Dream Big and Be a Dream Chaser

Building constructions have fascinated me since young. When there was construction in progress, I would spend the entire day watching the workers laboriously working on each floor in a new building from my balcony. Property development is both my hobby and investment vehicle, and I have built up a healthy portfolio over the years. Like everyone else, the aspiration to be successful in what I do drives my behaviour and attitude. A secret ambition for a long time was to achieve a doctoral qualification without sacrificing income. I wanted to achieve both career and academic ambitions. The workplace-based doctorate programme was a perfect fit. I am a jack of many trades and a master of a few.

Power behind the Dream

Friends often say my battery is super-charged because of the energy I put into my work and projects. My passion releases this energy. Discipline, a dare-to-try attitude, and hard work are my hallmark characteristics. However, passion and energy alone are not enough. Award recipients often pay tribute to their teams, spouse, family, and collaborators for their support behind the scenes. The power of leverage and team collaboration are often-used terms to encourage the concept that the whole is more than the sum of its parts. Collective power rather than singular effort is key to success. At my appreciation dinner, I thanked my team of partners, especially a small group of them who had gone through the 'thick and thin' of developing the business with me.

I can empathise with the devastating feeling of sudden unexpected obstacles when every inch of the being is devoted to chasing a dream. When someone trusted comes along and lends a helping hand, that support from authentic people is very impactful. We stand on the shoulders of giants and benefit from the bridges built by previous generations. On their shoulders, we see a bigger picture from a higher place and enable better decisions. Legacy is about building new bridges for the next generations to use and benefit from. I hope one of my legacies is about helping someone to become the next champion.

Life Paradigms and Values

My early work routines were predictable – long working hours punctuated by some social life and the occasional holiday. The focus in my career was achieving the first promotion, the next, and then the one after that. Bonus and salary increases were the highlights of a work year. Among friends at social gatherings, we would discuss a plateful of ideas solving many issues but never doing anything beyond the discussions. Sounds familiar?

Usual Life Paradigm Needs a Refreshed Mindset

The usual paradigm of most families is encouraging their children to *study hard, get a good job, work hard, save, buy a house, raise a family, aim for promotions, invest, improve lifestyle, and iterate the cycle.*

Of course, the sequence is not linear. I was doing all of that and at the same time, worried that not all may be well at retirement because of sudden disruptions which may cease employment. Such concerns exist irrespectively of people in employment or in business.

Much of the unrest in various parts of the world today is a result of people's inability to achieve their aspirations for a better life despite their willingness to work hard. The dream home is out of reach of most young people. Property speculations have resulted in many past financial housing bubble crises, and the fallout of the 2008 US subprime crisis was huge. Housing remains an important government agenda and various cooling measures to reduce speculative investments have been implemented to address these challenges.

More young people are opting to live at home while saving for their deposit. Their savings rate is lower than the rising property prices, which causes them to miss out owning their first property. Most governments have schemes to help first home buyers. Examples are Singapore's Housing Development Board (HDB) scheme and Australia first home buyers' grant. Clearly, the current paradigm to a better life needs a refreshed mindset.

Thinking Ahead and Foresight

Prof Vander Laan's framework on foresight style points out that the majority of the population are reactors and their characteristics include change resistance. Only a small population are framers, and the balance are testers and adapters. This explains why change management is so difficult despite the logic to change. People do not like to change unless they are forced. The curious people are likely to be testers and adopters. I fit the framers' profile due to my propensity to think long term and focus on the big picture. Framers need the support of testers and adopters to carry out the change agenda.

Figure 11.3 Foresight Styles

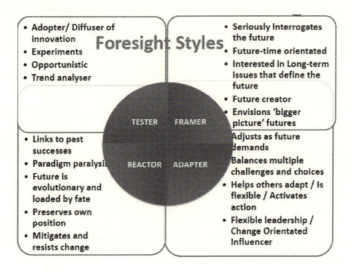

Source: Dr Luke Vander Laan

Work Hard

Today's workforce is encouraged to play hard as much as they work hard. My primary school's motto of work hard, play hard conveys the same idea. The attributes to success include working hard and authentic leadership. However, working hard does not guarantee career longevity, and therefore, the need for skills to keep pace with progress is vital for sustainability in this new world.

Work Hard and Become an Authentic Leader

Rising through the ranks in a corporate career is achieved through hard work and occasional wise decisions made. Career opportunities will surface when leadership believes in the employees' ability to deliver, their attitude to try, and their capability and capacity to serve. A trusted leader with followers is a result of authentic leadership.

I always remind my leaders that staff members are intelligent and that they can spot who is genuine or not. Being genuine nurtures trust. Being honest about limitations above broadcasting strengths is even more important. Having the guts to be accountable when outcomes are not meeting stakeholders' expectations is a challenge for any leader. I fought with my mind for some time when I decided to reduce my own income after a hard year's work when my division did not meet the planned goals. My self-talk included that I had worked hard, the results were not within my control, and personally, I did well. These were arguments I presented in my self-talk. In the end, I gave in to my leadership compass on accountability. It was a painful decision.

Another management principle is servant leadership. It is the concept that leaders serve and not the other way around. Gestures of respect and honour given to leaders are reasonable but should not get out of hand. Too many leaders love the gestures more than the responsibilities. They get angry or disappointed when the gestures are not accolated. Mother Theresa, who lived a humble life, was an example of true servant leadership. She served with great sincerity.

Authentic leaders serve with the attitude of what is best for the customer, staff, and society. They rule from their hearts and not just the mind. Take every opportunity to celebrate success. Attention spans are short, and the key is to grab the moment to celebrate the success with the team because the next *battle* is around the corner.

Having had the opportunity to live in multiple cities and working across cultures have led me to believe that the above principles are the same no matter what economies or cultures. Sensitivity to cultural nuances is key when working across borders.

I learned to focus on results and outcomes and live the missions I set for the organisation and for myself after years in leadership positions. My mission is to create and capture the value from opportunities and be realistic on timing on returns, as investments take time to nurture. The task of the leader is to balance both short- and long-term requirements.

Working Hard and Still Being Retrenched

It is important to remember that a leader is still a worker in the hierarchy of an organisation. Let me discuss work management from a worker's perspective. Five years into my initial career in Malaysia, I migrated to Australia in the late 1980s. I was introduced to many new business concepts such as enterprise transformation and restructuring. In came the world of retrenchments and job cuts as part of the transformation programmes. The reasons behind some of these transformations were to either arrest declining revenue or protect profits. The early retrenchment process was crude. Some staff would turn up at work on Friday as normal and then be called into a meeting room, where they would be told that they had been retrenched. They would be offered a package and optional counselling sessions. Obviously, many were shocked and psychologically unprepared for such news. Some were the sole breadwinner in the family and did not know how to live through the weekend or break the bad news to the family. Many of the scenes in the movie *Up in the Air* starring George Clooney reminded me of these learnings.

Management soon learns to better manage these programmes. Back then, I was told an employee could be retrenched as much as three times in a career lifetime statistically. Many of the affected workers have worked hard for the company in the past. Why would such a fate happen to them? The reasons are complex. Some point to the fact that the job roles have changed, and their skills are out of date. Productivity through automation has reduced the need for some jobs.

Work Hard, Relearn, and Reskill for the Future

The foresight style of tester and adapter encourages the worker to be a trend analyser, to experiment, adjust to changing demands, be opportunistic, and help others to adjust. They have to be open minded to change. The rate of change will be even faster going forward in the next two to three decades with the Fourth Industrial Revolution, where digital technologies will become more sophisticated thanks to artificial intelligence and machine-learning algorithms. The average worker cannot rely on knowledge learnt some 15 years ago at a tertiary institution. This is why workers need to continuously relearn and reskill to remain relevant.

Play Hard

Our Part in Social Responsibility

The Play Hard portion of my school motto was about holistic development of the child. Work hard and play hard is, therefore, not a new concept. The much-talked-about work-life balance in the 1990s to 2000s is about the workforce balancing between career goals and personal life. Today's organisational agenda is focused on superior performance, diversity, inclusiveness and impacts on society.

Back in 2016, world leaders adopted the 17 Sustainable Development Goals (SDG) Agenda for Sustainable Development[50] to address the global challenges related to poverty, inequality, climate, environmental degradation, prosperity, peace, and justice. It is a blueprint to achieve a better and more sustainable future for all. The goals interconnect and. in order to leave no one behind, the ambition is to achieve each goal and target by 2030 through the collective efforts of governments. The goals and call to action are summarised in the table below.

---

50 https://www.un.org/sustainabledevelopment/development-agenda/.

Table 11.1 United Nations Sustainable Development Goals (SDG)

	Goals	Challenge	Agenda	Call to Action
1	No Poverty	There are 836 million people who live in extreme poverty.	Economic growth must be inclusive to provide sustainable jobs and promote quality.	Donate what you don't use.
2	Zero Hunger	Over 1/3 of world's food is wasted.	The food and agriculture sector offers key solutions for development and is central for hunger and poverty eradication.	Avoid throwing away food.
3	Good Health and Well-being	There is a target of less than 70 maternal deaths per 100,000 live births by 2030.	Ensuring healthy lives and promoting the well-being for all at all ages are essential to sustainable development.	Vaccinate your family to protect them and improve public health
4	Quality Education	Over 265 million children are currently out of school and 22% of them are of primary school age.	Obtaining a quality education is the foundation to improving people's lives and sustainable development.	Help children in your community to read.

5	Gender Equality	One in five women and girls age between 15–49 have reported experiencing physical or sexual violence by an intimate partner within a 12-month period, and 49 countries currently have no laws protecting women from domestic violence.	Gender equality is not only a fundamental human right, but a necessary foundation for a peaceful, prosperous and sustainable world.	Call out sexist language and behaviours.
6	Clean Water and Sanitation	Water scarcity affects more than 40% of the world's population.	Clean, accessible water for all is an essential part of the world we want to live in	Avoid wasting water
7	Affordable and Clean Energy	The 13% of the global population still lacks access to modern electricity. Three billion people rely on wood, coal, charcoal, or animal waste for cooking and heating.	Ensure access to affordable, reliable, sustainable and modern energy for all	Use only energy-efficient appliances and light bulbs.

8	Decent Work and Economic Growth	The 50% world's population lives on US$2 a day. Global unemployment rates – 5.7% and having a job doesn't guarantee the ability to escape from poverty in many places.	Sustainable economic growth will require societies to create the conditions that allow people to have quality jobs.	Buy from green companies that are equal opportunity employers.
9	Industries, Innovation, and Infrastructure	Manufacturing value added per capita is USD100 in least developed countries compared to USD4500 in Europe and North America.	Investments in infrastructure are crucial to achieving sustainable development.	Think of innovative new ways to repurpose old material
10	Reduced Inequalities	Sixteen thousand children die each day from preventable diseases such as measles and tuberculosis.	Policies should be universal in principle, paying attention to the needs of disadvantaged and marginalised populations.	Raise your voice against discrimination.
11	Sustainable Cities and Communities	The 25% of urban residents live in slum like conditions.	The 60% of the world's population will live in cities by 2030. Provide access to basic services, energy, housing, transportation, and more.	Bike, walk. or use public transportations to keep our cities' air clean.

12	Responsible Consumption and Production	One third of food production is wasted. Households consume 29% of global energy and contribute 21% of resultant CO_2 emissions.	If the global population reaches 9.6b by 2050, the equivalent of almost three planets will be required to sustain current lifestyles.	Recycle paper, plastic, glass, and aluminium.
13	Climate Action	If no action, climate change will cause average global temperature to increase by 3 degrees.	Limit global warming to 1.5C global carbon emissions need to fill a staggering 45% by 2030 from 2010 levels	Educate young people on climate change to put them on a sustainable path early on.
14	Life below Water	The 20% of world's coral reef was effectively destroyed. Another 24% are imminently at risk.	Over 3 billion people depend on marine and coastal biodiversity for their livelihood	Avoid plastic bags to keep the oceans safe and clean.
15	Life on Land	The 20% of Earth's land area was degraded between 2000–2015. The 75% of world's poor are directly affected by land degradation.	One million plant and animal species are at risk of extinction.	Plant a tree and help protect the environment.

16	Peace, Justice, and Strong Institutions	Twenty million people are refugees. Over 41 million people have been internally displaced and 4m people are stateless,	Promote peaceful and inclusive societies for sustainable development, provide access to justice for all, and build effective accountable and inclusive institutions at all levels.	Use your right to elect the leaders in your country and local community.
17	Partnerships	Strong international cooperation is needed more than ever to ensure that countries have the means to achieve the SDGs.	Inclusive partnerships are built upon principles and values, a shared vision that place people and planet at the centre are needed at the global, regional, national, and local level.	Get the SDGs in Action app to learn about the goals and ways to help achieve them.

I believe all of us have a responsibility to read through these goals, respond to the call of action. and play our part.

Play Hard and Be Healthy

Besides social responsibility, students are encouraged to be involved in sports and extracurricular activities as part of wholesome development.

Like many people, I used to pay lip service to exercise. It was an agenda item on many New Year resolutions until it became a lifestyle routine ten years ago. My diet and eating habits were poor because of long working hours. Dinners were past 9pm, and suppers were frequent. As a result, my body weight and waistline kept increasing. I tried morning walks and then followed them with sumptuous breakfasts. The breakfasts neutralised the exercise efforts, and the weight problem persisted.

Badminton is one sport I played in my teenage years, and therefore, I enrolled in badminton training. I appointed myself as partner sponsor of this sport at work. With the changing of lifestyle, keeping my diet under control, and constant exercising, my weight is now under control and my waistline is managed. My health has improved, and I am now never too busy at work to sacrifice my health. If you were good in sports in your teenage years, use it to your advantage and participate in corporate sports and social activities. It helps to broaden networks and increase personal branding along the way. My CEO friend who joins us at social games occasionally says it is always refreshing to play with young people. Effective weight management comes down to a simple formula of output exceeding input. This is a simple daily reminder.

Janson at his weekly badminton session

Be Yet Wiser

Victoria Institution is one of the oldest secondary schools in Kuala Lumpur, Malaysia, where I grew up. Participation in extracurricular activities included joining a uniformed unit such as the school band or Red Cross. There was a list of societies and clubs to join. Students learned to manage clubs as roles were handed down from their predecessors, and teachers were assigned as mentors to provide additional coaching. Be Yet Wiser is the school's motto and the owl, which symbolises wisdom, is featured on the school crest. Much of the mindset and values learnt from these activities are foundations of my development.

Victoria Institution, Kuala Lumpur

Be Yet Wiser – an Alternate Paradigm

The future does not come to you. You help to create it. There is no one-size-fits-all answer. I had to choose what is best, given available time, commitments, aspirations, and capabilities. This alternative paradigm is to challenge and stretch multi-tasking capabilities instead of taking the linear approach. The objective would be to work on these work streams and deliver an integrated outcome that aligns with aspirations and dreams. Thereafter, it is a weekly task to monitor and work on the work streams in parallel.

Table 11.2 Life work streams, activities, and notes

	Work-stream		Major activity	Notes
A	Family	1	Function as a family	Love, respect, care, attend all events and celebrate all milestone
		2	Respect and supporting each other	Rooting for one another
B	Faith and Values	3	Belief	One's spiritual convictions and beliefs
C	Well being and health	4	Diet and exercising	Monitor one's health and well being
		5	Sports and recreation	part of social wellbeing and health
D	Social	6	Parties, gatherings and social	Network and social life
		7	Hobbies	Hobby is key to keeping one happy and relax
E	Personal	8	Grooming	keeping in shape and looking good
		9	Personal Brand	Do what you do best and high self esteem, actualisation
F	Education	9	Baseline knowledge expected of society	High School education
		10	Tertiary education	Vocational, Univ, Polytech, certification qual increasing
		11	In career training - top up	Continuous and cross discipline
G	Career	12	Job tenure	Full Time / Part Time / contract
		13	Job design	look for opportunities to explore different roles be careful to deliver within the assigned roles
		14	Other job opportunities	Have an open mind to explore
		14	Networking in Business or at work	Part of team, network and ecosystem
H	Expenditure	15	lifestyle and spend profile	Spend within budgets
		16	Emergency cash call	Build up reserve
I	Finance	17	Lifestyle	Plan for some savings and investment
		18	Savings and investment	Monitor and risk
		19	Risk Profile	Monitor risk appetite
		20	Perform lifecycle long term planning to understand Long term Cash Requirement Analysis	Simulations and scenarios of cash requirement throughout lifecycle
		21	Contingency cash requirement	Build up reserve
J	Investments	22	Long term superannuation fund	Build up reserve
		23	Invest with knowledge. Some risk needed	Track and monitor
		24	evaluate risks and insurance	Insurance coverage if needed
K	Charity	25	Give back to Society	Giving is earning and vice versa
L	Celebrations	26	Track milestones and celebrate. Mitigate if necessary	Take time to celebrate

I work with many young people in my organisation. Fresh out of university, they have dreams and ambitions. They want to work on interesting jobs, learn from mentors and coaches, and progress in their careers. Some dream of becoming the next iconic entrepreneur, Elon Musk or Jack Ma, and pursue their unicorn start-ups. Work-life balance is important to them. Environment and brand overtake pay according to feedback from some staff surveys. Their priorities quickly change once they reach 28–30 years old when they begin to settle down to start their families. Compensation becomes more important. The proposed alternate paradigm:

Work hard to acquire basic skills. Add to basic skills vocational and academic disciplines depending on one's makeup. Jobs can be contract or permanent depending on economic cycles. Practise frugal lifestyle. Save and invest. Top up skills constantly. Look for opportunities. Be part of society. Give back. Enjoy. Build a holistic career with family factored in the journey. Along the way, have health and wealth in check.

I encourage young people to start their financial plans early.[51] Some of the key elements include the following:

- Save a little a day and invest some of that savings.
- Lead a disciplined and frugal life to start the saving / investment cycle.
- Go for further out places if investment is property related so long as there is transport infrastructure. Government planning is always increasing regional communities to avoid over concentration in the city. Some young people want to invest in expensive areas at the onset.
- Protect the future – insurance, wellness, and savings.
- Build up a credit profile.
- Seek help where possible but be sure to have integrity in repayments.

With near-zero interest rates, savings as the main solution to wealth creation is limited. In some economies, there is a negative interest rate on savings. Risk appetite should be higher when you

---

51 Janson Yap, *Average to ACES*, 2019.

are younger because there is more time to recover. Adjust the risk appetite in the later part of life.

The usual paradigm of working hard to get ahead in life is a given but not quite enough. Young people face the dilemma of long working hours and having no time to pursue what they need to in order to prepare for their life ahead. A new alternate paradigm in pursuing career and life goals is important. The above table of 12 work streams helps prompt what needs to be worked on.

Be Yet Wiser – Be Open-Minded to Newly Opened Doors

Change brings new opportunities. Organisations need to embrace system-thinking strategy in this new digital era. Adopting an open mindset to reskill for the new types of jobs is an important attitude for career continuity.

Be Yet Wiser – Past Lessons Still Work

Dealing with difficulties hones character. There will always be pleasant and unpleasant situations. Responding correctly to unpleasant situations is a good opportunity to build character and personality. Allow me to share three life lessons.

Keep Cool No Matter What

I learned to keep cool from my days working in an Australian company. The New South Wales state business was the biggest contributor to the overall business in that company. Its general manager (GM) and his finance manager (FM) were known to be difficult colleagues to deal with. Our group marketing officer had challenges with this duo, as did many of us. All of us had to devise our workarounds to get work done.

I remember an incident where I threw up in the toilet after a meeting with the FM, which made me realise how upset I was. At another meeting, the entire management team was waiting for the GM to attend. My boss called him, only to be told that he was stuck in traffic. By then, the tension between him and many other management team members had reached boiling point. My boss went around the meeting room and asked each team member about their working relationships with this GM. The result was that the duo had to be retired. Keeping cool and calm in any situation has always worked for me.

Work on 3Cs of Attitude: Do Not Compare or Compete, Just Commit

Success is relative and what I deem to be success, others may not. Not comparing or competing helps. Avoid the keeping-up-with-the-Joneses attitude. This is an idiom referring to the comparison to one's neighbour as a benchmark for social class or the accumulation of material goods. I have seen too many frustrating situations and have much stress resulting from comparisons and competitions. It is futile. Having the right life attitude is vital to keeping mental soundness and blood pressure in check.

Commitment is willingness to give time and energy to a cause one believes in or a promise or firm decision to do something. Commitment leads to action. Action brings your dream closer to reality. Abraham Lincoln was quoted as saying, 'Commitment is what transforms a promise into a reality.' My commitment has always been to do my best according to my abilities.

Expect Bumps and Brakes

Obviously, there are heartbreaks, disappointments, anger, denials, and frustrations. There are bumps in the road, and sometimes brakes have to be abruptly applied. For some of these situations, I wish a different decision had been taken. The central theme of my other work, *Wow! How did you know that?* is about pre-empting risks and mitigating them before they occur. In some sense, we will never know if it did mitigate the risks because the issue did not materialise. But I would rather be safe than sorry.

Disappointing incidents and stressful moments are avoidable in a career over a long time. I wrote about working with difficult people. When I was still new at consulting, I was the manager in charge of a technology-assessment engagement with a subsidiary of a multinational corporation. My staff conducted the interviews and subsequently filed the report. The managing director of the local subsidiary summoned my staff and me to his office because he was unhappy with the negative comments in the report. The more my staff explained, the angrier he became, and he finally threw the report in my face. Both my staff and I were shocked and did not know how to respond. Luckily, I had learned to keep cool.

I also recall a professor in my undergraduate days who was famous for report throwing. Some people are bad at controlling fits of anger. Although I had these types of negative experiences, I also had many positive experiences of praise for work done.

The last two years have been stressful at work. Like any other large organisation, it is undergoing change and transformation. I teach Risk Management and Change. It is one thing to write and talk about *change* and another thing to live through the changes. I point to a quote in my book attributed to Rosabeth Kanter: 'Change is disturbing when it is done to us, exhilarating when it is done by us.'[52]

I had the opportunities to purchase two strategic properties at good prices, and I do regret passing up on these. One was my neighbour's house, and the other was at the back of my current property. In retrospect, I should have made the painful decision at that time to commit and tough it out. I was quite debt leveraged and did not dare to commit new risks. While there have been misses, I can point to a number of properties I invested in that made good capital gains. Equally, not all property investments are gems; there are duds as well. A couple of condominium and office/unit investments did not turn out to be what was promised and ended as poor assets. Losses were quickly realised.

---

52 Yap and Nones, 'Wow! How did you know that?', 2018.

With bumps in the road, we must find ways to lift our spirits whenever we feel vulnerable or downcast.

The Total Package of Who I Am

Irrespective of what success paradigm I have followed in my journey, my family has always been totally supportive of what I do to pursue my dreams and goals. This support from my family has been essential for all my pursuits to date. I have worked with both the usual and what I call the alternate paradigm of success. Value is both quantitative and qualitative. My assessment is that both paradigms have both created and captured value at different levels. Some are more visible and therefore easier to measure.

Table 11.3 Paradigms to success

Paradigm	Core idea
Usual	*Study hard > get a good job > work hard > save > buy a house > raise a family > aim for promotions > invest > improve lifestyle > and iterate the cycle*
Alternate	*Work hard to acquire basic skills > add to basic skills vocational or academic disciplines depending on one's makeup > jobs can be contract or permanent depending on economic cycles > frugal lifestyle > save and invest > top up skills constantly > look for opportunities > be part of society > give back > enjoy > build a holistic career with family*

I started with the usual paradigm to success, the paradigm I was brought up to believe, and I achieved most of my Maslow needs such as stability in my financial situation, decent qualifications, a stable family, and a successful professional career. Looking back, I achieved good self-esteem as a valued professional, a social network, and enough financial resources to meet lifestyle needs. I have worked and lived in four major cities in ASEAN and have travelled around the world as part of my work. My wife has made sacrifices in terms of her own business career while my children have had the benefit of broader cross-cultural exposure and education while living in two of the four cities. I started my monthly commuting routine ten years ago when we decided that it was time for the children to focus on their higher secondary schooling, prepare for university, and establish their own social networks.

The alternate paradigm that I devised, based on my own experience and learning, has enabled me to achieve breakthroughs and new levels of outcome. This positive mindset is reassuring in many ways. My improved self-worth and self-esteem have reduced self-doubts and negative self-talk. I stay relevant by topping up skills and knowledge through continuous learning. New academic knowledge generated through my research is shared for the greater good. Future generations are benefiting from the mentoring and sponsorship programmes of my foundation.

One of my criteria is whether others assess my outcomes as ace and whether my work is rewarded. Collectively, I would judge my journey as ACE.

I Am Ready for More

It is time to unleash the power within. The next S Curve has commenced. Let me share with you the lyrics of the song, 'I am ready for MORE.' It is my attempt to describe my thoughts for my next life adventure.

All the best.

12.0

I Am Ready for MORE

#More Ready

In speaking with many of my friends in retirement, they have approached this topic mainly from a financial perspective. Stress, a sense of loss, or dissatisfaction left them filling the day with whatever activities that came along. This chapter discusses my experience of addressing transition and the future in an integrated framework.

What is next for human beings after Earth? Space is the next frontier. I met Colonel Eileen Collins, a retired female astronaut at our annual Deloitte Southeast Asia Partner Conference when writing this chapter. Meeting her was a rare treat, and her story was inspiring. She was invited to share her career testimony. The moderator introduced her as the first female commander of a US spacecraft in 1999 and the first astronaut to fly the space shuttle through a complete 360-degree pitch manoeuvre. Her mission was to test safety improvements and resupply the International Space Station in 2005. Back in the 1990s, aviation was a male-dominated industry. Her profile, experience, and iconic leadership fit nicely with the conference theme, which was Leading for Legacy, Moonshot 2023. As a career woman and mother, she also fits the inclusiveness and diversity agenda of Deloitte.

Her passion and intellectual capacity to overcome social norms demonstrated that nothing is impossible. Life is about choices. She subsequently retired from NASA in 2006 to spend more time with her family and pursue other interests. I did ask for her views around career transition. She said, 'Take time to wait for the next opportunity if circumstances permit. There is no rush.' Wise counsel.

Many Transitions throughout the Life Cycle

Each life stage can be represented as a sigmoid (S) curve, where the start of a stage is at the bottom of the S pointing to a commencement phase then moves along the upward gradient of the S signifying the growth phase and eventually plateaus off unless its cycle is interrupted. The challenge for business is the optimal time to interrupt a growth curve before it reaches its peak. The intersection of the two S curves is what researchers call the chaos zone. It is the period when the current phase is coming off its peak, at the top of the current S, and the next phase starts, which is represented by a new S. Indeed, my mental and emotional state had been *chaotic* over the past few years as I was contemplating life after retirement and at the same time trying to optimise current career opportunities.

Book stores are well stocked with self-help books, and many are written to assist the boomer generation, that is those born between 1946–1964, to cope and prepare for their post career lives. People in this generation are either in retirement from their career or close to retiring. With a longer lifespan and the retirement age pushed back to later years, the consistent theme of these books is to encourage the boomer to relook at their employability and keep themselves active. Books like *Retire Retirement* by Tamara Erickson and *Generation Cherry* by Tim Drake are good reference materials. *Generation Cherry* is a metaphor for a generation looking for things to do like a second bite of the cherry.

JY World Stage 2.0: Future

The theme of 'the future of X' is dominating many seminars, journals, and publications, each trying to claim a space about the future ecosystem and landscape. The X label includes common contemporary topics such as banking, finance, mobility, and the list goes on. There are many programmes aimed at informing the participants and stakeholders on what the future looks like and how to prepare to be ready for this future.

There is a concern that what worked previously might not work in this new digitally disrupted, competitive landscape. Strategists are advising organisations to rethink their strategies, refocus their innovations, and reframe their transformative efforts. Organisations must learn new skills, assess whether their foundations can be leveraged, and execute on new competitive strategies.

Transition Strategy

I have participated in different committees to address preparations for the future both at work and in community programmes. A common question asked is what I would be doing in the next five to ten years while helping others think and plan for their future. As I reflected on these conversations and worked through my transition, my strategy development process touched on many components and work streams.

Components of the Transition Strategy

There are six interconnected components in the transition-strategy framework. Strategy development is not a linear process and while I list the components in an order; it is not intended that each component is worked through in a linear way. The diagram below describes my framework, which features six components.

Figure 12.1 Components of JY World Stage 2.0, Transition and Future Strategy

Dreams and Passions

The hope for happiness and dreams of a better future are goals for most people. Those who are passionate about chasing their dreams find enormous energy to execute the tasks, no matter how laborious they are. The smile on the face, the joy in the heart, and the satisfaction in the mind tell it all when dreams and passions are achieved. Dreams and passions bring like-minded people together, and they tend to work well together because of their common objectives. Respect and solid relationships are developed through good teamwork, and support for each other is often seen through this oneness in spirit.

Sports competitions illustrate the above point well. The dream to be the ultimate champion releases the personal drive, which pushes every muscle to train and reach the peak of form. The support and encouragement of family and friends are important to help sustain the sports athlete's long and lonely journey towards the championship.

Concerns

While pursuing dreams, feelings of anxiety exist. In a survey of top retirement concerns, 85% of Americans experience financial anxiety. They are concerned about insufficient savings for retirement or outliving retirement savings and that they may become a financial burden[53] to others. It is observed that anxiety has increased over time according to a Northwestern Mutual study.[54] Humans are creatures of habit and routines. Depression creeps in when an individual feels he is no longer important or as occupied in a post-retirement environment. This is especially so if self-esteem and self-worth are built around titles, scope of responsibilities, accolades, deadlines, meetings, and deliverables. Fear of loss is cited as a concern or source of anxiety in another study.[55] Losing someone to death in addition to the feeling of lost ability to do the things we were once able to do are sources of concerns.

My list of concerns as I approach my next lifecycle is similar to the ones observed above. They include:

1. addressing my financial situation post active income
2. having views and feelings of self-worth and self-esteem
3. maintaining health and wellness
4. interacting with communities and relationships
5. maintaining an active lifestyle
6. defeating inner enemies

The main contributing factor to most of the above concerns that lead to anxious feelings, loss, and disappointments can be summarised in one word – insecurity. Melanie Greenberg, who wrote in *Psychology Today*, points to the perfectionism mindset as a cause of

---

53 'The Top 5 Retirement Concerns', *The Retirement Manifesto*, 20 September 2016.
54 Ibid.
55 '6 Retirement Concerns that we're thinking about today', canadianbudgetbinder.com, 23 April 2019.

insecurity. Some set their standards too high and, despite their best efforts, the outcomes do not measure up to this yardstick. The results include constant disappointments and blame for being anything less than perfect, leading to feelings of insecurity and unworthiness.[56] Her prescriptions include: (1) controllable effort invested versus outcomes that have external factors beyond control, (2) evaluate whether the extra effort to achieve perfection is worth it, and (3) close to achieving a goal is good enough.

Security is the opposite of insecurity, and its definitions include fixed, positioned, or successfully addressed threats. By successfully working through the different components in the strategy framework, fulfilment and satisfaction increases, thereby positively improving the sense of security.

- *Financial planning*

Since financial anxiety is a big concern, sizing the nest egg in a post-retirement environment is important to ensure that there are sufficient funds available for use when career income ceases upon retirement. Most financial planners begin by helping clients establish their future target monthly-spending level to determine the size of the nest egg. To avoid a drastic drop in spending pattern, some use 70% of current income or spending level as a guide in the computation. Ben Fok in his article on the basics of retirement planning uses the table below[57] to simulate the size of funds needed at the time of retirement.

In the example below, the nest egg of $600,000 will be depleted in 18–23 years after retirement based on a 3% annual investment growth rate and an expenditure of about $3,000–$3,500 monthly.

---

56 Greenberg, 'The 2 Most Common Causes of Insecurity and How to Beat Them', *Psychology Today*, 6 December 2015.
57 Ben Fok, 'Getting down to the ABCs of planning for retirement', *The Sunday Times*, 27 October 2019.

Table 12.1 How many years will your nest egg last?

Nest Egg value	Monthly usage	Annual Drawdown rate	Annual Investment Growth Rate									
			3%	4%	5%	6%	7%	8%	9%	10%	11%	12%
600000												
	6500	13%	8	9	9	10	11	12	13	15	17	22
	6000	12%	9	10	11	11	12	14	16	18	23	
	5500	11%	10	11	12	13	14	16	19	25		
	5000	10%	12	13	10	15	17	20	26			
	4500	9%	13	14	16	18	22	28				
	4000	8%	15	17	20	23	30					
	3500	7%	18	21	25	33						
	3000	6%	23	28	36							
	2500	5%	30	41								
	2000	4%	46									

Source: Grandtag Financial Consultancy

Once the nest egg value is computed, the task of accumulating this value is the biggest challenge. It may take years to accomplish this goal, and it should be started as soon as possible.

FIRE is an acronym describing a niche-lifestyle movement to achieve financial independence and retire early. This desire to be rich and retire early is the dream of many, but few achieve it. However, as the article suggests, this movement has gained in popularity in recent years.[58] The concept is simple. Get the highest pay possible and save along the way. Channel the savings into investments, and when the income from the income-yielding assets achieve the targeted active income levels, one can retire.

- ***Self-worth and self-esteem***

Sometimes defeats and setbacks can dent confidence, leading to doubts around self-worth and self-esteem. In more severe cases, depression sets in and becomes an issue of mental health. The concern with fast-paced change that is happening in the world is that people who cannot adapt and cope with the change may experience mental

---

[58] Koh Ping, 'How to be retire before 40, Chong Invest', *The Sunday Times*, 27 October 2019.

and psychological stress. Likewise, for retirees, psychological stress may arise with a sense of loss in self-esteem because there are no more offices, responsibilities, reporting lines, and titles.

Therefore, having a healthy perspective on self-worth and self-esteem is important to maintain positive mental wellness. Just remembering past achievements without ongoing achievements or new goals may be detrimental to self-esteem. Therefore, set new goals and pursue them.

• *Health and wellness*

Health is not completely within one's control. Healthcare expenditure can be significant. The goal is to stay healthy as long as possible. Many life-threatening diseases can be managed if detected early. Lifestyle and self-control play a key part in either delaying onset of diseases or managing the severity of the conditions. Governments worldwide are also very concerned about spiralling public healthcare costs. Government agencies have devised many programmes to move the healthcare value chain from treatment and recovery centricity to prevention and wellness centricity.

Despite advances in medical science, humans must also play their part. My learning is that regular exercise throughout life has significant health benefits. Consciousness of lifestyle choices and diet together with setting some wellness goals early in life are important. A common mistake is giving into entertainment, corporate dinners, and no time for exercise, increasing risks of lifestyle diseases.

• *Communities and relationships*

Humans are social beings. One of the disadvantages of a busy career is the amount of time spent at work. The communities and relationships may end up mostly work and career related. When circumstances change, one may feel a loss because these work relationships will no longer be the same.

Therefore, it is important that executives have a balanced view of their different communities and relationships, no matter how busy they are at work. Invest in quality family relationships and lasting friendships outside work so that social life and the sense of belonging are not compromised when work is disrupted. Tamara[59] rightly pointed out that one of three key retirement strategies is to explore and develop good relationships. Test the quality of the relationships and networks so that they can prove useful at the right time.

- *Active lifestyle*

An idle mind leaves room for unhelpful self-talk. If lifestyle changes significantly, particularly from busy to idle, there would be concerns. A productive routine adjusted to cope with the physical condition and the maintenance of an active lifestyle help to avoid the challenges of an idle mind. In my transition year at work, my schedule did change significantly, and it has taken some months to adjust. This highlights the need to think through how to gradually adjust schedules and still perform meaningful activities that have productive outcomes.

- *Inner enemies*

Often, personal challenges appear to be bigger than they really are. Avoid instant reactions to challenges. If time permits, take time to reflect and talk them through with trusted friends. Dealing with the issues after some cooling-off time invariably creates a better result unless the issues are time sensitive. Defeating inner enemies by having a realistic perspective on challenges is another tool to positive mental health. My Christian faith has proven useful in defeating past inner enemies. I am sure this trust in God will still be needed when dealing with my future challenges.

---

59 Tamara Erikson, *Retire Retirement*.

Capabilities and Personality Make-Up

Each of us is different in our capabilities and personality make-up. An honest periodic SWOT assessment is like a good check-up on oneself. Why is personal SWOT analysis helpful? It allows a person to reflect on each component and drive different programmes to improve either capabilities or accept the limitations and try one's best to optimise opportunities. Sometimes the feedback may be hard to accept and dealing with some of these assessments needs courage.

Figure 12.2 SWOT

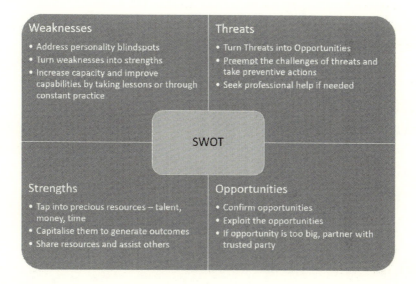

Let us work through two examples on threats. If health is a concern, proactively seek a timely medical assessment on health matters and adjust your lifestyle in line with the assessments. If the threat is financial, then seek help in long-term planning and short-term measures to get ahead of the game. I advocate good financial planning throughout life. Sometimes business and personal opportunities do pop up. Seek counsel to confirm that they are genuine opportunities and exploit them for benefits.

Weaknesses can be turned into strengths through training and remedial plans. Continuous learning and reskilling can strengthen weaknesses. In a circular economy, be generous with your resources of talent, money, and time. Share some of them for the greater good. Better things may come your way.

Foundations and Platforms

There is no Fourth Industrial Revolution without the first three revolutions. Capabilities, competencies, and capacities are developed over time. An experienced surgeon owes his skills to his undergraduate training as a medical student. Unless something drastic has happened which requires someone to forgo past foundations, it is almost imperative that one:

A. leverage foundational learnings
B. explore and develop networks
C. combine hobbies and skills for new products and vocations
D. develop a personal brand and image

Most people use their hobbies for personal interests, relaxation, and social purposes. In retirement, one can combine hobbies and skills to create new products. Some might even be able to use these products for commercial gain. All of us are known for who we are. It is our brand image, and we are our own brand ambassadors. We should not go from top of brand to loss of brand just because we retire. Without faking it, do your best to maintain your usual grooming habits. There is no need to give your wardrobe away upon retirement.

Life Stage

We move into another life stage at retirement. At 60, or thereabouts, other changes besides work patterns are likely to occur such as becoming in-laws and grandparents. There will come a time that current roles, responsibilities and accountabilities will change.

It is good to read and understand how best to capitalise of these realities, adapt, and modify behaviours and activities and reap the benefits.

Future Environment

As said earlier, the components in this framework are interconnected. There are different aspects of the future environment to be mindful of when addressing the transition strategy. They include:

1. having a worldview
2. understanding the impacts of the new environment, which is often characterised as volatile, uncertain, complex, and ambiguous (VUCA)
3. knowing what Industry 4.0 is and some of the trend factors
4. understanding how digital and human factors coexist
5. living with smart devices everywhere

The world of the Fourth Industrial Revolution in an age disrupted by technological development (digital) coexist with humans. Having a world view and understanding the big picture are important. Think global and act local. Dream big and act small. Be a system's thinker by thinking holistically and working out which components one can capitalise on through SWOT assessment and determine an appropriate response.

We have covered all six components of the transition strategy. In summary,

C. know the future environment
D. have dreams and passions to spur life on
E. Deal with life concerns
F. use SWOT to address some weakness while turning threats to opportunities to improve capabilities.
G. understand your personality make-up

H. build on foundations and platforms
I. accept your life stage and respond accordingly

Doing the Right Thing or Doing It Right

Doing the right thing is described as strategic thinking. *Doing it right* is tactical thinking or execution. Both are important. Strategy execution is just as important as strategy formulation. The value of the strategy is about the degree of fitness between the company and its environment. The linear approach in strategy is often three steps including analysis, formulation, and execution in a closed loop as shown below:

- Environment – analysis
- Strategy – formulation
- Company – execution

In the age of digital disruption, agile execution is even more important. Strategy becomes a continuous process and often requires continuous tuning of the strategy along the way. As such, strategy *learns* from what the company executes and from feedback from the environment (market). The company *builds* through the strategy execution while the environment *measures* the performance of the strategy and execution.

- Environment – analysis – measure
- Strategy – formulation – learn
- Company – execution – build

Figure12.3 Strategy process in the Disrupted Age

Strategy as a process
Lean Startup

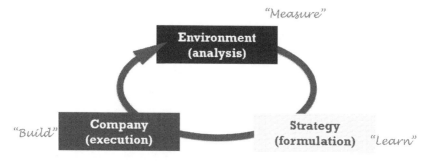

Source: INSEAD, SDD, 2019

Traditional views of strategy adopt the aim, ready, and fire approach and then repeat the whole cycle. Today, it is more about aim, ready, fire, and then repeatedly ready and fire with alignment against the target along the way.

Fresh Mindset: Four Autonomies Needed

Formulating and executing the strategy by taking the right steps, activities, and process form part of the answer. There is no perfect strategy, neither can one execute the strategy flawlessly. The bigger challenge is to have the right mindset to approach the future. Tim Drake wrote about a fresh mindset for a fresh opportunity. Building a sense of autonomy helps to achieve the aspirations of the dreams and purpose and be the person one wants to be.

The four autonomies are earning, learning, giving, and recharging.[60]

---

60   Tim Drake, *Generation Cherry*, RedDoor, Glasgow, UK, 2017.

- Earning: Even with provident fund or pension, a little extra income makes life comfortable. It is about being plugged into society and keeping oneself connected to work.
- Learning: Learn, do not wilt. Keep the mind engaged.
- Giving: Giving back is immensely rewarding. It means participation. It strengthens self-worth.
- Recharging: Participate in activities that are engaging and enjoyable. They are relaxing and have the effect of recharging our life batteries.

Besides developing the right strategy, executing it well is equally important. The right mindset for execution is key.

Risk Intelligence and SMART

In an unstable environment, the exact execution of any planned strategy is unlikely. A new risk intelligent strategy called SMART methodology includes sensing, mitigating, aligning, remodelling, and transforming. The sensing element is to sense the environment and mitigate the risks of execution. There are many types of risks such as financial, health, and environment, which if pre-empted can be successfully mitigated. In the VUCA world, the strategy has to be aligned or realigned depending on the changes in the environment. With this alignment, the goal is to remodel and transform my future portfolio to produce a new targeted income stream. Besides income, there are other plans for new health and lifestyle models.

MORE READY

The research and design of the future workplace, process, and structure as well as interactions between the workforce are ongoing. The evolution and revolution will bring new demands on today's talents and much of the above discussion goes into the preparations along the way. I am convinced that young people on joining the workforce should be taught the dynamic changes that are happening as well as some of the components which take decades to address.

I invested some time in addressing what being more ready for the future means for me as I confront my own transitions. To sum it up, I share my MORE READY framework.

Table 12.2 MORE READY

M	Marketability	Improve my image and brand as a leader and consultant.
O	Opportunities	Constantly look out for opportunities while focusing on delivering the present. Evaluate the opportunities carefully.
R	Resources and Relationships	Build up the arsenal of resources just like a reserve bank would build up its assets. Explore and build on quality relationships.
E	Energy and Exercise	Exercise is a must and a priority. Release energy on purposed activities.
R	Regret-less	Take timely decisions and think whether I would regret later if I did not act. Be less regretful in the future by being more proactive in decisions requiring my talent and assistance.
E	Experiment and Esteem	Be not afraid to experiment. Some of these outcomes build self-esteem.
A	Aim for ACES	Aim for some outcomes to be acknowledged and rewarded as good and awesome.
D	Dreams and Desires	Do let the fire burn and continue to dream. Pursue rightful desires.
Y	Youth Mindedness	Be young in mind and attitude.

Thank you for reading Average to ACES. Are you ready for MORE? I am.

Janson recording one of his songs

I am ready for MORE?

Lyrics: Janson Yap, Kent Tonscheck
Melody: Kent Tonscheck

A new sunrise, future has arrived
And it's better than I ever thought I'd see
I've forgiven and I learned from the trials in my life
And treasured the best of memories

Verse 2
Decades passed, decades yet to come
Years have flown but I never felt younger
My eighties will feel like forties again
I'll take own time to enjoy the wonders, but

Chorus
I am ready for more
This world and this life, promises to explore
Now, trust in it and live life right
Believe and come along for the ride
Because I know, I know, I know, I know that
I am ready for more
My hindsight guides my foresight
Stars line up on a beautiful night
The futures brighter than it's ever been before
I know, I know that x3
I am ready for more!

Verse 3
I'm looking forward to what's to come
I'll speak the words in my heart
And I'll fly to new heights on wings of courage
Youthfully chasing desires

Chorus

Verse 4
My God, the praise of my life
Can teach me more than I could ask
Life will bow, with my friends surrounding
We will celebrate the highs, singing

Chorus

After several weeks of writing, the inspirations keep evolving after attending each service.
Thank you, God. Inspired at church service, 5–12 May 2019. Revised on 25 June 2019.

Appendix

Key expected events in Decade 2020 to 2030

Sports events
2020 Summer Olympics in Tokyo, Japan
2021 SEA Games in Hanoi, Vietnam
2022 Winter Olympics in Beijing, China
2022 FIFA World Cup in Qatar
2022 Commonwealth Games in Birmingham, UK
2023 SEA Games in Phnom Penh, Cambodia
2024 Summer Olympics in Paris, France
2025 SEA Games in Thailand
2026 FIFA World Cup in Canada, Mexico and the United States
2026 Commonwealth Games
2027 SEA Games in Laos
2028 Summer Olympics in Los Angeles, USA
2029 SEA Games

Elections
2020 United States elections
2021 Singapore Parlimentary election at the latest
2023 Malaysia GE15
2024 Indonesian Election
2028 Indonesian Election

AEC
2025 AEC Blueprint: ASEAN Forging Ahead Together

Significant buildings
2020 Jeddah Tower
2020 New World Trade Center

Space
2020 China 3rd space station
2021 James Webb Speace Telescope
2022 European Space Agency launch JUICE exploration of Jupiter
2023 SpaceX sends private citizen on a lunar free return tourism mission
2024 SpaceX launch a human mission to Mars
2025 Giant Magellan Telescope
2026 Solar eclipse

Infrastructure
2021 Red Line of the Tel Aviv Light Rail
2022 first Indian bullet train between Ahmedabad and Mumbai
2024 Fehmarn Belt Fixed Link between Denmark and Germany
2025 Singapore Smart nation

China
2020 China 3rd space station
2030 China 4.0

References

AFP News. "Blasts at Sri Lanka hotels and churches kill 156." 2019.

Amadeo, Kimberly. (2018, November 6, updated 2020 March 17). Stock Market Crash of 2008. Retrieved from The Balance: https://www.thebalance.com/stock-market-crash-of-2008-3305535

Amadeo, K. (2019, January 20, updated 2019 June 25). Hurricane Harvey Facts, Damage and Costs. Retrieved from the balance: www.thebalance.com>hurricane-harvey-facts-damage-costs-4150087

Amadeo, Kimberly. *How Does Obamacare Work for Me?* 12 March 2019. <https://www.thebalance.com/how-does-obamacare-work-3306053>.

—. *Stock Market Crash of 2008.* 6 November 2018. <https://www.thebalance.com/stock-market-crash-of-2008-3305535>.

AskStart. "Connecting the unconnected." *Science section.* Singapore: The Straits Times, 27 April 2019.

Bernanke, Ben, Hank Paulson and Tim Geithner. *Bernanke, Paulson and Geithner: revisiting the 2008 financial crisis.* 29 May 2019. <https://www.theguardian.com/business/2019/may/29/bernanke-paulson-and-geithner-revisiting-the-2008-financial-crisis>.

Campbell, Charlie. "Leveraging 5G." 2019.

Cassidy, John. "Ten years after the start of the great recession, middle class incomes are only just catching up." 2018.

CFE. *Report of the Committee on the Future Economy*. Singapore: Government of Singapore, 2017.

Christman, Ed. "BillBoards's Money Makers: The Highest Paid Musicians of 2018." 19 July 2019. www.billboard.com.

Drake, Tim. *Generation Cherry*. Glasgow, UK: RedDoor, 2017.

Egstark. *How is Obamacare paid for?* n.d. <http://money.com/money/collection-post/4537027/how-is-obamacare-paid-for/>.

"Fukushima Daiichi Accident." n.d. *World Nuclear Association*. <https://www.world-nuclear.org/information-library/safety-and-security/safety-of-plants/fukushima-accident.aspx>.

Gordon, Lydia. "The recovery from the Global Financial Crisis of 2008: Missing in Action." 2014.

Kamarck, Elaine. "The fragile legacy of Barack Obama Boston Review, April, 2018." April 2018. *Boston Review*.

Metzl, Jamie. *Making babies in the Year 2045*. Singapore: The Sunday Times, 2019.

National Academy of Sciences. *Summary - Lessons learned from the Fukushima Nuclear Accident for Improving Safety of US Nuclear Plantrs*. Washington (DC): National Academies Press, 2014.

Pearlman, Johnathan. *He came, he saw, empty bushland, he built a city*. Singapore: The Straits Times, 2017.

Senior Supervisors Group. "Risk Management Lessons from the Global Banking Crisis of 2008." 2009.

Svitek, Patrick. "Gov. Greg Abbott: Texas ready for next Hurricane Harvey." 6 June 2018. *texastribune.* <https://www.texastribune.org>.

United Nations ESCAP. *Ageing in Asia and the Pacific: Overview.* Bangkok: United Nations ESCAP, 2017.

van der Zee, Dana. *Smart Nation Singapore.* Kingdom of the Netherlands: Holland Innovation Network, 2017.

Wakefield, Jane. "Christchurch shootings: Social media races to stop attack footage." 2019.

—. "Christchurch shootings: Social media races to stop attack footage." 16 March 2019. *BBC.* <https://www.bbc.com/news/technology-47583393>.

Yap, Janson and Nelson Nones. *Wow! How did you know that?* Singapore: Gadwise Investments Pty Ltd, 2018.

Zilber, Ariel. "United States will drop to become the world's third largest economy behind China and India by 2030, new financial rankings suggest." 2019.

Index

A

ACES ix, xiv, xvii, xix, xx, xxi, 46, 49, 52, 69, 83, 99, 107, 116, 128, 143, 147, 151, 168, 189
Affordable Care Act 9, 10
Ageing 32, 197
Ambition xiv, 3, 24, 30, 48, 68, 105, 119, 153, 154, 159, 167
Ange Dove ix, xviii, 118
Art 39, 59, 71, 72, 73, 74, 75, 76, 77, 81, 82, 88, 119
Aspirations 39, 107, 111, 151, 153, 155, 166, 187
Australia xii, 14, 30, 38, 85, 87, 92, 148, 155, 158
Authentic Leader xiv, 157
Average ix, xvii, xxi, 15, 141, 147, 148, 159, 163, 168, 189

B

Badminton xii, xvii, 48, 49, 51, 52, 56, 57, 58, 60, 62, 63, 64, 66, 67, 68, 71, 74, 75, 101, 105, 106, 107, 108, 109, 110, 111, 112, 114, 117, 135, 165
Branding 101, 113, 122, 165
Breakthroughs 24, 26, 65, 85, 91, 96, 97, 98, 106, 153, 173
Business Model 15, 26, 119, 125, 126

C

Change xix, xx, 6, 7, 13, 22, 26, 31, 43, 126, 139, 140, 141, 149, 150, 151, 155, 156, 159, 163, 168, 169, 171, 180, 181, 182, 184, 188, 189
China 1, 2, 3, 4, 22, 25, 32, 33, 37, 44, 129, 130, 131, 132, 138, 193, 194, 197
Connections 11, 26, 85, 124
Contemplations 66, 68
Crossroads xx, 44, 100, 108, 109

D

Daphne Ng ix, 100, 111
Decade xi, xx, 5, 6, 7, 10, 11, 12, 13, 14, 19, 20, 21, 22, 23, 25, 26, 28, 31, 33, 150, 159, 189, 191, 193
Dedication 3, 52
Defining Moments 5
Deloitte xi, 73, 76, 129, 131, 137, 174
Digital Connections 11
Digital era 5, 7, 169
Diligence 102, 104, 148
Discipline 58, 81, 100, 102, 104, 154, 168, 172
Disruptions xii, 6, 7, 25, 26, 93, 155, 186
Dream xiv, xxi, 3, 4, 29, 46, 52, 68, 69, 81, 83, 85, 86, 87, 89, 90, 93, 99, 116, 119, 128, 143, 147, 151, 152,

153, 154, 155, 166, 167, 168, 170, 172, 177, 178, 180, 185, 187, 189
Dr. Janson Yap ix
Dr. Lim Cheok Peng ix

E

Economic Crises 7
Education xii, 7, 26, 31, 38, 39, 41, 42, 43, 48, 60, 73, 78, 96, 103, 118, 135, 148, 153, 160, 173
Enemy 56, 59, 60, 63, 178, 182
Entrepreneur xi, xiii, 118, 120, 123, 168

F

Family xiii, xvii, 2, 3, 4, 7, 30, 39, 41, 45, 48, 49, 51, 52, 75, 78, 79, 88, 101, 108, 110, 116, 124, 129, 130, 131, 132, 136, 137, 138, 139, 147, 152, 153, 154, 155, 158, 160, 168, 172, 175, 177, 182
First break ix, 3, 85, 86
Foresight vii, xii, 23, 155, 156, 159, 191
Fukushima Nuclear Plant 7
Future vii, xx, xxi, 2, 3, 4, 5, 6, 8, 12, 14, 20, 22, 23, 24, 25, 26, 29, 31, 33, 42, 43, 46, 47, 69, 73, 76, 77, 82, 83, 98, 99, 100, 101, 108, 109, 111, 115, 116, 119, 128, 131, 143, 153, 159, 166, 168, 173, 174, 175, 176, 177, 179, 182, 185, 187, 188, 189, 191, 196

G

Gao Li ix, 4, 129
Global Financial Crisis 15, 20, 196
Globalisation 29
Goals 49, 52, 62, 66, 67, 68, 77, 91, 100, 101, 107, 108, 109, 111, 131, 139, 157, 159, 160, 164, 169, 172, 177, 179, 180, 181, 188
Good Values 44

H

Healthcare 2, 3, 9, 31, 32, 37, 38, 39, 40, 41, 42, 43, 141, 181
Heart 24, 41, 157, 177, 191
Heroes xix, xxi, 58, 153
Hope xix, xx, 3, 24, 25, 29, 65, 66, 76, 80, 81, 113, 154, 177
Human beings 1, 174

I

Industrial Age 5
Industrial Revolution xix, xx, 6, 11, 27, 149, 150, 159, 184, 185
Industry 4.0 xii, 11, 185
Injuries 3, 52, 57, 63, 64, 65, 66, 104, 115
Innovation xi, xx, 30, 162, 176, 197
INSEAD xii, 187
Interconnectedness 26
Internet xx, 11, 12, 21, 25, 26, 27, 28, 120, 124, 127, 149, 150

K

Kayak 11
Kent Tonscheck ix, 85, 87, 98, 191
Knowledge xii, 3, 39, 40, 42, 59, 96, 97, 110, 112, 120, 127, 128, 159, 173

L

Leader xi, xiii, xiv, 2, 6, 39, 106, 157, 158, 159, 164, 189
Learnings vii, xii, xiv, 6, 23, 31, 33, 41, 44, 56, 58, 62, 64, 67, 82, 97, 106, 121, 127, 138, 150, 151, 158, 159, 173, 181, 184, 187, 188
Legacy xiii, xxi, 6, 7, 9, 37, 39, 41, 42, 46, 69, 83, 99, 116, 128, 143, 154, 174, 196
Love xiii, 45, 61, 68, 71, 72, 81, 90, 91, 92, 95, 105, 116, 127, 128, 152, 157
Lucky break 85, 86, 96

Lyddia Cheah ix, 47

M

Management xi, xii, xiii, xv, xix, 8, 15, 25, 31, 37, 39, 42, 56, 109, 124, 155, 157, 158, 165, 169, 170, 171, 197
Mastery 53, 102
Mindset 59, 96, 155, 166, 169, 173, 178, 187, 188
Mission xxi, 31, 41, 46, 69, 83, 99, 116, 128, 143, 147, 158, 174, 194
MORE ix, xii, xx, 5, 7, 8, 11, 12, 13, 15, 19, 20, 21, 22, 23, 24, 25, 26, 30, 32, 39, 40, 42, 43, 44, 47, 48, 52, 54, 57, 58, 59, 62, 67, 72, 73, 86, 88, 92, 96, 97, 98, 101, 102, 107, 108, 109, 110, 113, 115, 116, 120, 122, 123, 125, 126, 127, 130, 131, 132, 135, 136, 137, 138, 139, 140, 141, 151, 154, 155, 157, 159, 161, 162, 164, 168, 169, 171, 172, 173, 174, 175, 180, 181, 186, 187, 188, 189, 191, 192
Music 38, 85, 88, 90, 91, 92, 93, 95, 96, 97, 98

N

New Reality 12
Next Stage 109, 115
Noah Tan ix, 70, 71
Nuclear Disaster 7

O

Obamacare 9, 10, 195, 196
Opportunities 31, 43, 78, 89, 96, 107, 118, 120, 121, 131, 132, 135, 139, 140, 157, 158, 168, 169, 171, 172, 175, 183, 185, 189
Organisation xi, 31, 39, 78, 82, 107, 113, 114, 158, 167, 169, 171, 176

P

Paradigm 23, 30, 151, 154, 155, 166, 168, 169, 172, 173
Passion xii, xiv, xxi, 2, 37, 40, 41, 45, 46, 54, 60, 67, 69, 70, 71, 82, 83, 86, 88, 89, 95, 99, 100, 101, 105, 110, 111, 116, 128, 143, 147, 153, 154, 174, 177, 185
Peace ix, 11, 129, 159, 164
Physical xvii, xx, 5, 7, 12, 28, 29, 56, 62, 126, 131, 161, 182
Pioneer 28, 37, 40, 74, 80
Platforms xiv, 7, 12, 86, 101, 108, 126, 128, 184, 186
Play hard 151, 156, 159, 164
Potential xix, 13, 95
Power xx, 12, 25, 27, 32, 56, 60, 110, 122, 153, 154, 173
Professional athletes 3, 58
Progress ix, xix, xx, 5, 25, 57, 62, 66, 98, 129, 140, 142, 153, 156, 167
Purpose ix, 68, 90, 96, 109, 111, 129, 137, 141, 184, 187

R

Rainbow Centre 71, 72, 73, 74, 75, 76, 77, 78, 79, 81, 82
Ready ix, 4, 8, 33, 60, 70, 72, 78, 86, 91, 96, 118, 148, 173, 174, 176, 187, 188, 189, 191, 197
Recession 15, 18, 19, 20, 21, 123, 125, 196
Reflections 2, 46, 56, 59, 61, 69, 79, 83, 90, 99, 104, 107, 116, 128, 143, 151, 152
Refreshed 155
Relearn 159
Reskill 149, 159, 169
Resources 8, 11, 89, 96, 113, 130, 151, 152, 153, 172, 184, 189
Rethink 176

Retrenched 158
Risk Intelligence 188
Rooting 151, 152

S

Self-worth 61, 173, 178, 180, 181, 188
Sharing Economy 6, 12, 31, 126
Singer 3, 85, 88
Skill xx, 31, 42, 45, 53, 54, 56, 60, 62, 70, 71, 73, 77, 80, 97, 112, 121, 125, 140, 148, 150, 156, 158, 168, 172, 173, 176, 184
SMART 12, 27, 30, 31, 57, 150, 185, 188, 194, 197
Social Responsibility 112, 159, 164
Soniia Cheah ix, 47, 64
SOSG 73, 74
Space 26, 27, 28, 29, 118, 119, 126, 174, 175, 194
Sports 53, 54, 55, 56, 57, 61, 63, 64, 66, 67, 73, 75, 100, 101, 102, 103, 104, 105, 106, 109, 112, 115, 135, 138, 164, 165, 177, 193
Stock Market Crash 14, 15, 16, 18, 19, 195
Story xiv, xvii, xviii, xix, xx, xxi, 1, 2, 3, 4, 52, 70, 86, 92, 101, 116, 141, 142, 147, 151, 174
Strategy xii, xix, 27, 53, 59, 67, 68, 107, 109, 169, 176, 177, 179, 182, 185, 186, 187, 188
Success vii, xiii, xviii, xix, 26, 38, 40, 41, 42, 43, 47, 52, 56, 57, 60, 67, 68, 69, 86, 91, 92, 96, 102, 104, 113, 139, 142, 147, 151, 152, 153, 154, 156, 157, 170, 172
Support xvii, 3, 32, 40, 41, 47, 52, 53, 57, 66, 74, 76, 78, 79, 81, 82, 89, 92, 121, 152, 153, 154, 156, 172, 177
Survival 131, 133, 135
SWOT 107, 108, 111, 183, 185

T

Technology 4, 5, 6, 7, 11, 12, 24, 26, 27, 31, 56, 57, 93, 110, 118, 124, 126, 127, 141, 142, 150, 159, 171, 197
Transformation xii, xix, 6, 7, 25, 26, 139, 140, 158, 171
Transit 76, 135

U

Unconnected 27, 28, 195
Unique 52, 59, 81, 92, 135

V

Values xxi, 30, 31, 32, 33, 40, 44, 46, 69, 82, 83, 93, 99, 116, 122, 125, 128, 143, 147, 151, 154, 158, 162, 164, 166, 172, 180, 181, 186
VUCA 12, 185, 188

W

Wiser xiv, 140, 151, 165, 166, 169
Workforce 31, 150, 156, 159, 188, 189
Work Hard 105, 151, 155, 156, 157, 159, 168, 172
World Stage xxi, 1, 47, 71, 108, 151, 175, 177

Made in the USA
Monee, IL
19 March 2022